carry

all.

REVERSE
Jesus Ruiz, Untitled

I used to carry it all.

edited by
Marjie Bowker

STEEP STAIRS PRESS
Edmonds, Washington

Published by
Steep Stairs Press
23200 100th Ave W
Edmonds, WA 98020
steepstairspress.com
425.431.7270

Cover art by
Jesus Ruiz

Copyedited and designed by
Tim Holsopple
Armored Bear Creative
armoredbear.co

LCCN
2024905639

ISBN
978-0-9974724-4-8

BOOKS PUBLISHED BY STEEP STAIRS PRESS

1	*We Are Absolutely Not Okay: Fourteen Stories by Teenagers Who Are Picking Up the Pieces*	2012
2	*You've Got It All Wrong*	2013
3	*Behind Closed Doors: Stories from the Inside Out*	2014
4	*We Hope You Rise Up*	2015
5	*I'm Finally Awake: Young Authors Untangling Old Nightmares*	2016
6	*This Is a Movement: Owning Our Stories, Writing Our Endings*	2017
7	*Listen: Young Writers Reflect on Chaos, Clarity, Action, Balance*	2019
8	*This Smile Is for Everyone Else*	2021
9	*I Used to Carry It All*	2024

Kathy Clift and Joan Jett at Scriber Lake High School (2012)

Dedicated to Kathy Clift (1952–2023)
Scriber Lake High School Principal (2003–2015)
Champion of Scriber storytelling since the beginning

"As I have come to know Scriber students, I am convinced that they are 'children of promise' who just need a safe place to continue the hard work they have already begun. They are resilient enough to show up and move forward. I hope their stories build a bridge to more understanding and dialogue."
—from *We Are Absolutely Not Okay* (2012)

CONTENTS

WHY WE WRITE

These are stories we thought we might never tell. They have been on the tips of our tongues since the events occurred.

To write them down, to publish them, and to read them out loud is like finally finding the word you've been thinking about all day. It feels like relief; you can move on with your sentence, your day, and your life.

Carrying our stories was a constant discomfort. Publishing them feels like putting the weight down—a missing piece to our healing journey that will allow us to take hold of the future.

We hope others will be able to find a way to put their burdens down through relating to our successes and sorrows.

You don't have to carry it all.

OPPOSITE
Jesus Ruiz, Untitled

MIRROR MIRROR

Andrew Barnes

I am the quarterback, and I just led my team to a win against the best team in the league. Celebration, cheers, and the smell of sweat fills the locker room as I change back into my tennis shoes, shorts, and T-shirt. I look in the mirror and see broad shoulders and no hip dips. Most importantly, my boobs are gone; my chest is flat with slight pecs.

I see myself the way I am supposed to be, how I want everyone else to see me.

I feel normal. Myself.

Beep! Beep!

My alarm went off and I jerked up.

Shower time.

I stepped into the bathroom and looked in the mirror that stretched out and covered most of the wall. An overhead skylight made darkness impossible.

I began to take off my white undershirt, revealing my belly button, then my torso. After a deep breath and slight hesitation, I pulled the shirt up over my chest and over my shoulders.

Gazing into the mirror brought back the familiar pain, obscuring everything in my dream.

I was only half naked and I already felt like a stranger to myself. My hip dips, my chest, and my arms—the things I hated most about myself—jumped out at me, so I tried to focus on the things I liked: my broad shoulders, my somewhat fit torso, and the mole below my belly button.

I forced my eyes back to my chest, but this time everything went blurry. When I made eye contact with the person in the mirror, I saw red and puffy eyes and tears running down my cheeks. I leaned against the wall and slid down slowly. Disappointment scattered through me with strain. My stomach hurt.

I can't take it anymore.

I balled my hands into fists while my legs shook.

I felt brave for allowing myself to look at my upper body, but weak for not being able to handle it.

I couldn't even think about looking at the rest of my body—I wasn't ready to face that. I picked myself up, walked out of sight of the mirror, and finally took my pants and boxers off. I stepped into the shower.

Rage coursed through my veins, like someone was holding me back, keeping me from fighting with myself.

Why did I have to be born this way? Why does my body make me doubt the fact that I am a boy? I know I'm male enough, but why does my body have the right to make me feel less about that?

Growing up, I refused to wear dresses and dreaded trying on anything feminine. I always wore the masculine clothing when I played dress-up with my siblings. During shopping trips, I would look longingly at the boys' section. One time my mom caught me and said, "Do we need to go over there? If you want a boys' bathing suit, just say so." But I was too afraid to let her down, so I said, "No," and then tolerated the girls' section.

I wasn't consciously aware that my gender was the problem until puberty hit—that's when the football dreams started, and my hatred for what the mirror revealed became unbearable.

~ • ~

The summer after eighth grade, I found myself leaning up against the bathroom counter, staring in the mirror again, noticing every detail of my face: acne and red blotches of eczema, glossy green blue eyes, the redness in my cheeks, freckles on my nose, the ginger hair covering my eyebrows, and the smile I have faked in so many pictures at church.

After taking it all in, I spoke words out loud to the mirror-person that seemed to have no meaning:

"You're a girl."

I thought about all the times I have been asked, "Are you a boy or a girl?" and how the question always shook the whole inside of my body.

Keeping eye contact with my image, I spoke the word, "She."

The word made me cringe and jump in my skin.

Trying again, I said, "They? Them?"

These words didn't feel as unsettling, but still—they didn't feel quite right, either.

Hesitating before trying once more, I barely whispered the word, "He."

Goosebumps.

That felt right.

It was what I had been seeing in myself that I hadn't been quite able to describe. As I stared at my reflection, my eyes started to water. I asked myself, "Are you a boy? Does that feel right to you?"

I didn't have to answer the question. In my heart, I knew it was right.

With adrenaline flowing through my veins, I stepped out of the bathroom. Then I stopped with fear.

I will disappoint everyone.

I'll mess up not only my relationships with my friends but also the relationships they have with theirs.

Even with that fear, I felt tired from wearing the mask of someone else for fourteen years. I knew it was time to take it off and stop hiding.

~ • ~

A few weeks later, with my secret still in place, I was shooting baskets at the end of our cul-de-sac. With the burnt orange ball in my sweaty hands, I felt the trace of leather through my fingers.

I jumped and let the ball fly from my hands, then heard the satisfying thud of the backboard. The ball went through the hoop and the net swished. I ran to the ball feeling the crisp breeze through my hair. I went for another shot, feeling calm adrenaline flow through my body.

My inner monologue started as I continued to shoot. The voice was calm and deep, but soft at the same time.

There isn't always tomorrow, so why haven't you taken the jump? Why haven't you let yourself live?

As the ball left my hands again, I thought about having a whole life in front of me to live.

Why waste it now?

With a deep sense of certainty, I decided: I am going to be myself. The boy I have always seen myself as.

When I thought about what the future might hold and what it might mean for me, my mind started to wander back to everything that had held me back:

The voice of my mother: "She's not trans, she's just very masculine."

The voice of people I once called friends: "Ew, did you hear about that one girl who thinks that she's a boy?"

The voices of strangers: "Trans people will never be like us."

My own voice of fears: "I'll never be enough. Nobody will ever love someone like me."

I tried to shake off those thoughts as I put all the negative energy I felt into shooting the ball. I made a few more shots, then went inside and put all of it in the back of my mind.

I'll let it resurface someday.

~ • ~

Within a week, I sent a text to my best friend, Emma.

I gotta tell you something.

I couldn't believe I was about to do it; I was about to tell her the biggest secret of my life.

carry it all.

Her name popped up on my screen seven minutes later.

I'm here, what's going on?

Without hesitating, I wrote:

I think I'm trans, I've known for years but didn't have the courage to accept it.

She asked some questions—questions that make me feel safe and understood and helped me open up more.

I hate my chest. When I look in the mirror I just want to rip it off and never have to see it again.

I literally can't stop smiling. You're figuring yourself out and I'm so happy for you. At first I was sitting in shock. But thinking about it, it all makes sense now.

The fear of losing my best friend went away and feeling her support meant the world to me. We texted about names for me, clothing, and redecorating my room. She decided on my middle name: Greyson. She said she had always wanted to name her son Greyson.

You'll be Uncle Grey to my kids in the future!

We agreed that when the time comes for her to have kids, I'll be their Uncle Grey.

~ • ~

Within another week, it was time to tell my parents.

My dad was sitting in a blue- and white-striped rocking chair in the living room when I got up the courage to say, "Dad, there's something I need to tell you."

"Okay," he answered with concern. When I hesitated, he asked, "Is what you're about to tell me a bad thing? Should I be worried?"

"It's not bad; at least, it shouldn't be. But I don't know how you'll react," I answered. I realized how much I wanted to just say "it's not a bad thing" but couldn't.

Is it a bad thing?

I tried to speak but couldn't. My throat was knotted up and wouldn't let any words out. Finally, I said, "I have written a letter. I'll give it to you since I'm not able to say it."

I went upstairs to grab it but while looking around my room I couldn't find it. My eyes began to burn as my tears expressed what words could not. My hands were shaking, and my stomach felt like it was doing cartwheels; my heart just hurt, like ropes were tied around it and the ropes were getting tighter and tighter. I started going through my journals to find a clean page to write in when out fell the note I'd already written. After reading it again, the fact I was still hiding filled me with rage. I picked up the letter and ripped it until I could no longer rip it into any smaller pieces. I let water from the bathroom faucet run over the pieces, then threw the damp mess of paper away so it could never be read again.

I sat at my desk and cried for the next forty-five minutes until I heard my dad's gentle knock on the door. He came in, sat on my bed, and said, kindly, "What's going on? What do you need to tell me?"

Hesitation hit again before I could finally let everything out. I told him how I felt about my body and what led up to the realization. I told him I wanted to change my name.

He just sat and nodded, taking everything in. Finally, after listening for an hour, he said, "Well, you know I will always love you. Actually, I don't know what took you so long—I have known for about three years now."

His statement was comforting, but also made me wish I had told him sooner.

~ • ~

I switched school districts in the middle of the pandemic and started ninth-grade Zoom School as "Andrew." No one knew me, and I didn't ever turn my camera on, so I was completely anonymous. I planned to go "stealth"—I didn't want to tell anyone the details of my life. During a class discussion, though, another student mentioned wanting to get top surgery. Without thinking much about it, I sent him an email letting him know I was trans, and that he was not alone.

When I showed up in-person for hybrid school, no one knew. I passed easily from the moment I made the transition. Soon, though, I told another classmate whose sister also happened to be trans, and I told my English teacher. I was shocked that they both gave such positive responses, and this made me want to reveal more. I started going to a gender therapist and was diagnosed with gender dysphoria. I started working with a hormone doctor to stop my period and began to consider starting testosterone.

And just like that, I was no longer internalizing the transphobia I felt toward myself.

~ • ~

Just as I was easing into feeling comfortable in my own skin, I was caught off guard while eating a sandwich with my friends during breakfast period. We were just messing around and laughing with one another when a tall, muscular guy at the table stopped the conversation, looked at me, and asked, "It's none of my business, but are you male or female?"

I froze. Then quietly, with no confidence, I answered, "I'm male."

When I turned away from him I heard one of my friends say, annoyed, "His name is Andrew and he uses he/him pronouns."

"Yeah, I know his name is Andrew," he said.

Shame and doubt overtook me.

Is my voice too high right now? Do I need to lower it?

Although my clothes were baggy, I became super self-conscious of my chest and my curves. Things I hadn't thought about much since coming out in what seemed to be a safe atmosphere.

Later he approached me during the passing period. My heart filled with panic; I was afraid he was going to attack me. After identifying as female for so many years, it was still surprising to me when guys would randomly come up to me and say things like, "Yo Andrew, what's up bro?" while fist-bumping me, punching me, picking me up, grabbing me, and just touching me.

But he didn't touch me. He said, "Hey man, I just wanted to apologize for what I said. It wasn't cool of me and man, I'm just new to the game so like I didn't mean it. I just didn't know."

The apology was nice, I guess, but a part of me hated that he called it a "game." Maybe he just didn't know the right choice of words. One thing I knew for sure was that he was being a jerk earlier. He knew my name and my clothes covered me.

It's not a joke.

It's not a game.

It's a scary experience for almost every trans person.

It can be life-threatening.

~ • ~

These days, getting dressed requires extreme mental preparation. Before putting on my binder each morning, I think of the pain it will bring during the day—how hard it will be to breathe, and how it will dig into my rib cage. If I don't wear it, I'll be constantly thinking about my chest and how visible it might appear. I usually tackle it as quickly as I can. Sometimes I dread the simple act of speaking because my voice is not the way I want it to be. Although it isn't painfully high, it still sounds like I'm a prepubescent twelve-year-old boy, and I have to focus on masking it every time I talk.

But I either do these things or deal with the haunting ghost of dysphoria surrounding the private parts of me: The feeling of going into a competition that you know you're guaranteed to lose. The feeling of discomfort like walking in water with socks on. The feeling of constant disappointment.

My struggles with the mirror continue. I still feel like looking at myself is illegal—as if I'm looking at someone else and they don't know it. Like my head is mine, but the rest is a disconnected piece of me I just carry around.

Another struggle is the jealousy I feel toward other people who don't have to deal with these things. People take for granted that they can look in the mirror and see the correct gender looking back at them, and that they don't have to consider surgery to make things right.

When I talk to my image, I say, "You got this Andrew. You are stronger than you think. This binder, this dysphoria, and everything else in your head isn't going to change that."

This self-talk gives me energy to keep going. This, and a simple future vision that means everything to me:

> I'm walking down a West Seattle street leading to Alki Beach. It's fall, the sky is blue, and the leaves are red and yellow. Everything is balanced and fresh. When I reach the sand, I take off my jacket and feel the cool breeze on my skin. When I unbutton my short-sleeved Hawaiian shirt and the breeze hits the scars on my chest that mark my battles and surgery, I feel a sense of relief; all that I have gone through hasn't been for nothing. I feel proud. All the doubt and fear of going through with the process of transitioning has been worth it. All the doctor appointments and therapists have been worth it. I know that the little boy I once was is so proud of me for doing the very thing he wanted to do for years: step on a beach and feel the breeze against his bare chest.

Just over a year ago I was afraid to hope, but today, I rest in the knowledge that all of this will be worth it.

A NOTE FROM ANDREW

When Marjie asked me if I wanted to write my story, I was on edge about it. I didn't know how it was going to turn out or if it was going to have an impact. When I started writing, I continued to have doubts that my story meant anything, and I thought that it wasn't as important as other stories were. It was sometimes difficult to put myself back into situations where I didn't feel most comfortable, but it was nice to unpack my experiences and describe how I felt. I wrote about my story in the hope that others who are questioning or dealing with the same feelings and emotions know that they aren't alone. I also hope my story will help others who may not have a good understanding of what it's like for a trans person.

As for where I am now, I hope to start testosterone in the future and just continue to grow as a person. I think mentally I am more confident and at ease, and as days go by I feel more and more comfortable with myself. One of my friends once told me, "Things may be rough, but nothing is permanent, so keep going." That statement was an eye-opener. Yeah, life can suck, and it may take a while for it to get better, but in the end—whatever situation you're in—there will be light.

As a trans person fighting with body image and self-worth, I have come to realize that I love my body as much as I hate it: I love my thighs while I hate my hip dips, I love my boxy build while I hate my chest, I love my eyes while I hate my face, I love my personality while I hate my voice. I know that I have worth in this world, and I know that it's okay for me to take up space, but when society tells me otherwise it's hard to fight for and believe in myself.

carry it all.

OPPOSITE
Jasper Rhodes, Untitled

SHADOWS AND A BRIGHT WHITE LITTLE LIGHT

Olive Burk-Poole

My dad pulls away and puts his hands on my face, his eyes still watery. "I love you, Baby," he says. "I hope you know that. I love you so, so much. And you're making me so proud, you're making your mom proud. You're so strong for doing this. I'll miss you, Baby."

I cry even harder at the mention of my mom and fall back into his arms.

"I love you too, and I'm really gonna miss you. I'm sorry."

"Don't be sorry. There's nothing to be sorry about," he answers.

The all-white hospital room with the cold metal roll-up door fills with melancholy. I pull away and look at the stretcher.

This is really happening. I finally did it.

I get on the stretcher and lie down, and as a nurse places my stuff underneath I notice her name tag. *Olivia.* The name I disowned. My *real* name.

"Hey, we have the same name!" I say cheerily.

"Oh, that's cool! I haven't met another Olivia!" she says.

It makes my heart flutter, then fall and break. *How sad. The first other Olivia she meets is a patient she's taking to a psych ward.* But I simply smile back as the gathered staff start to push me to my fate.

"I love you!" I yell to my dad as I look back at him.

"I love you too," he says.

I can feel his heart cracking more and more with each syllable he speaks. His face is even more red than it usually is, making him look like a leaky fire hydrant. As I am rolled farther and farther from him, I can still see the wrinkles on his forehead from his furrowed eyebrows.

I don't want to see him in any more pain.

Slowly I turn around and lie back on the stretcher, watching as nurses and doctors walk past me on their way to other patients' rooms. The realization continues to grow.

I'm going to the psych ward. I'm going to the psych ward. I'm going to the psych ward. I'm only sixteen and I'm going to the psych ward.

The final doors open and I'm outside being led to an ambulance that will take me to Mary Bridge Children's Hospital, my home for the next week. A few of the nurses lift the legs of my stretcher, lock it in place, then roll me into the ambulance. One nurse hops in and sits on a metal bench behind me while Olivia closes the door and gets in the driver's seat.

"Do you want anything from your bag for the ride?" a nurse asks in a modulated voice, which brings me some comfort. I request my Pagan book and he looks through my bag and holds it up for me to confirm. I start reading the book and quickly get lost in the pages, thinking about how this moment might be spiritually enlightening.

As my eyes finally close and I drift into a deep sleep, a feeling of bliss and peace runs over my body, telling me that it's okay, that I'm forgiven. Even though I'm asleep, I can sense that I'm moving. The air cools, making the heaviness of the blanket feel even more comforting.

But the undercurrent of big change sends knots to my stomach. Nothing is gonna be the same after this.

Bumps on the road shake me awake, making me once again aware of where I am. I toss and turn, wanting to fall back asleep until I make it to the hospital, but the straps start to burn my skin and scream at me to look and think about what I've done.

I look through the window of the ambulance. *I'm so sorry, mom.* I can't believe everything has gone so wrong without her, or how quickly everything fell apart. Shit was already bad when she was alive, but her passing destroyed any sort of security I had. I can imagine how much better things would have been if she were still alive. Would I have gone to that party? Would I have done all the terrible things I did at skate night? Would I have run away in a drug-induced rage? Would I have become a filthy druggie?

~ • ~

Brownish beige walls surrounded me as I sat on my mom's worn couch with my dad, brother, and grandpa.

Two months had passed since I returned home from sixth-grade camp and learned about my mom's terminal brain tumor. My mom had been dealing with cancer for four years and various addictions for more than twenty. But the brain tumor was a death sentence. For those two months, my whole family—my dad, brother, mom's parents, and her sisters—were together at my mom and her boyfriend's house waiting for the clock to stop ticking, trying to get her to talk about what she wanted for her passing. She wouldn't do it, though. She would not admit defeat.

When Stephan, my mom's boyfriend, came upstairs and called my dad over, I knew.

"Terry, it's Whitney . . ."

No . . . It can't be!

My dad stood up, patted me and my brother on the shoulder, walked toward the stairs in the kitchen, then headed down. My face grew hot as my eyes filled with tears, making it impossible to see. But I already knew what had happened. Nothing more needed to be said. Time came to a standstill as every inch of me fell apart. My hands began to shake uncontrollably.

When my dad came back up the stairs, his eyes were red and puffy.

No no no no no no no no.

He walked over and sat down between my brother and me.

"She—she's gone . . ." he said.

In one moment, my reality shifted. The woman who had given me life . . . her life had ended.

"No, no, she can't be!" I yelled.

My dad nodded as my grandpa began to weep—the first time I'd ever seen him cry. Tears started pouring down, cooling my hot face.

My cries got more and more frantic as grief settled into its new home. Stephen called the medics to come and take her away. I didn't go down to see her. By the time the medics came, we had settled down a bit. We weren't completely calm, but we had started to accept our fate.

An EMT walked through the front door, said a quick hello, then headed downstairs. Red and white lights flickered out of the corner of my eyes; I turned around to see an ambulance parked outside of our garage.

Just as I looked out the window for one last glimpse of my mom, four medics came out of the garage carrying her on a stretcher. They put her into the ambulance, closed the doors, turned off the lights, and drove away.

The last time I will see my mom is on a stretcher . . . She can't be gone! Not yet! She was supposed to stay! She was supposed to be here for me! Stop! Come back with her! I wish I had gone down the stairs. I wish I had gotten to see my mom up close just one more time before they took her.

Once the ambulance drove out of sight, we all fell into each other's arms, screaming, crying, grieving together.

~ • ~

After my mom died, an emptiness loomed deep within my stomach, an emptiness so big I felt like a ravenous animal in a locked room with no food.

It was big the night my nana and I took my aunt and seven-year-old cousin, Scarlet, to the skating rink. They were visiting from California, and I wanted to do something fun with them.

"I can't wait to go skating with you, Olive!" Scarlet squealed, looking eagerly at me with ocean-blue eyes and rosy, freckled cheeks.

"I can't wait either! You're gonna look so cool with your pro skater cousin!" I answered with a slight chuckle. I was trying to be present with her, but I was already too far gone. My mind was in a completely different space. When I spent time with my nana or my aunt, all I wanted to do was ask questions about my mom. I hoped that each answer would bring me closer to her, but instead the answers just reminded me how far away I truly was. I was sure that the gap would never close.

When we pulled into the parking lot, we were greeted by the familiar big orange sign with a red curved arrow that read Lynnwood Bowl & Skate, also known as "the place you can find me every Friday night from 7 to 11." Ever since my mom's death, I was always getting high either out on the rink or out by the gazebo.

"What size are the quad skates and what size is the inline skate?" the lady at the counter asked.

"A size 8 and a size 10, please," I replied.

She nodded, walked over to the huge shelves of skates, and grabbed our sizes.

"Here you go. Enjoy!"

We grabbed our skates and headed back to our booth to put them on. As I fastened each strap, feeling them grip me tight around the ankles, I saw a man standing by the snack bar. He was really tall and wore sweats, a T-shirt, and a blue zip-up hoodie. He seemed more like a thing, a figure, a shadow. But very familiar.

I had known him for years, but he had morphed into something no one could recognize anymore. His name didn't fit the new him, so he went by a new one. His face didn't fit the new him, so he changed that, too. Before anyone realized what was happening, the person we knew had disappeared.

No matter where I looked, he was there, an overwhelming presence that was off-putting and dark. But something called me to him. I didn't know what was so alluring, why he had me in such a grasp. I tried to shake out of it by skating with my cousin, but each second I spent ignoring the man and his dark presence, he only seemed to grow bigger. He was all I could think about.

"Hey guys, I'm gonna say hi to one of my friends," I said, looking over at my family. "I'll be quick."

I shoveled through my bag for whatever money I had and headed over to the shadow. He greeted me by saying, "Aye, what's up man, how you been?" I almost didn't see a distinguishable figure in front of me; instead I saw a mist with fog that closed in, making the air thick and hard to breathe in.

"Hey! Nothing really, I'm just with some family right now." I tried to make small talk to make it seem like I was actually saying hi to an old friend, but really, I was meeting a new one.

"That's cool, that's cool. You looking to buy right now?" he asked.

"Uh yeah, I heard you got Xans? How much are they?"

"Five dollars a pop—but if you buy five you'll get 'em cheaper." A smirk grew on the shadow's face as I fell deeper and deeper into his trance.

"Alright. I'll buy five then."

"Good shit. That'll be $20."

We traded money for drugs, then I put the baggie into my pocket. When I looked up, the shadow was gone, nowhere to be found. I continued to skate with my cousin and enjoyed my time with her until closing. It was my first night at the rink without weed, because I didn't want to be inebriated around my family.

We all piled back in the car to go home. When we pulled into my nana's driveway and went inside, we all went our separate ways to get ready for bed. My Aunt Olive got Scarlet ready for bed while my Aunt Erika made the couch comfy for her. I went into the bathroom and, with the flick of a switch, four bright yellow walls surrounded me and my hot pink backpack. It felt strange to be in my childhood bathroom, because it felt like everything was about to be different forever. The pills were calling.

I changed into my pajamas and said goodnight to my family, then laid down on a foldout bed and waited for them to fall asleep. As soon as it was quiet, I sneaked back over to the bathroom and turned the light on again.

The walls seemed even brighter than before.

I locked the door and shuffled through my bag until I felt the tiny resealable bag. I pulled it out of my pocket and stared at the pills.

Wow, I can't believe I actually bought these. I wonder what it's gonna be like?

I was excited to try something new. I had heard good things about the effects, and I felt I needed something to occupy the emptiness in my mind.

I opened the bag and the yellow walls faded to black; all structure in the room was gone. The room didn't have a visible end. I was in the middle, alone with my little baggie. The shadow was back and bigger than I ever thought it would be, swallowing the entire house, leaving me to my demise.

Suddenly a sink appeared. The Xanax was shining bright in my hand, making it impossible to not notice. *It's too late now.* I turned the faucet on and put my head underneath it to get enough water to swallow the bright white light.

~ • ~

I carried this bright white light inside me. Everything around me started to whittle and rot away as if a parasite was taking over everything. The light was so bright I couldn't see it for what it was: destruction.

Slowly, everything fell apart in front of my eyes. My dad and I started getting into verbally abusive fights. I was getting high on weed everyday—risking everything just to be a little stoned—and getting so drunk I could barely even stand up. I regularly stole things from the mall, got put in the back of a cop car, and couldn't keep anyone around for longer than a few months. My best friend and I had a falling out. I was feeling more alone than ever.

One night I was invited to a back-to-school party by a friend. I didn't know anyone at the party very well, but I didn't care. A group of people were singing "Happy Birthday" to a guy standing in the center of the circle, and I was singing along with them, even though I had no idea who he was. Everyone was smiling, laughing, smoking cigarettes, and rolling on Molly, mixing it with other substances and feeling amazing. After standing around and shooting the shit for a while, we all started getting a bit cold. Some people were heading inside, but I stayed outside because I didn't want to deal with what was going on in the house. The boy I had been trying so hard for was all curled up with another girl, and I didn't quite want to admit that I still wanted him to love me like nothing happened. After standing outside for what felt like hours on a cool September morning, I was shaking violently from the morning drinking and coming down off cocaine.

As I took a drag from the cigarette, I felt a weird energy behind me. I turned and saw a guy sitting in a chair. "Hey sweetheart, you look cold. Take my jacket," he said. He took off his leather jacket and handed it to me. I hesitantly took it as I glanced into the house to see the guy who I *wished* was handing me his jacket. I had known him for two years, and he had been sending me signals all night, but all for nothing. I couldn't think straight.

Taking this other guy's jacket felt like betrayal.

"Here," the guy said as he pulled me toward him and put me on his lap, "for extra warmth." As a cigarette passed around amongst us and others, his hands started moving around my body. He told me how attractive I was and how *fun* I looked. He kept treating me like a little toy, saying teasing things and touching me all over. Earlier, I told my friend that I thought he was attractive, but now I was surprised by how uncomfortable I felt. There was something about him and his silver tongue that made it impossible for me to escape.

"We should go inside. Does that sound good?" he asked. I softly nodded my head, dozing off, out of my mind. I stumbled as he guided me down the hall, keeping me very close. I heard him say, "Two in 24 hours." But I was focused on not puking. When we got to the bedroom, there was no one there. "Perfect," he said under his breath.

My memory of what happened next is fragmented. I remember throwing up. I remember him making me continue. I remember seeing two people at the door; one of them was the guy I wanted to be with. When I made eye contact with him, his face fell apart. The pain I saw made me snap back to reality.

What am I doing?! Why am I doing this?!

Then, my questions for the universe turned into hatred, for myself and for him.

I hate you! You ruined it! You're a terrible person! I HATE YOU!

The door closed almost as fast as it opened, and once I realized no one was going to stop this, I got locked out of my brain again. When I came back into consciousness, he was done and I was clothed.

We walked out of the room with his hand around my hip. "Yo! Just scored two in 24 hours!" he exclaimed to the people in the living room. Feeling less sober than before, I mindlessly followed his every step like a puppy. I was trapped.

After a while, the party died out as people went home. The remaining few lay on a couch, and I was stuck under his arm as he laid behind me. I could feel the eyes of the boy I wanted, his heartbreak filling the room, building up tension so high my head felt like it was going to explode. My guilt grew stronger with each quick glimpse at his face.

Finally my dad texted, asking me to send him the address so he could pick me up. After texting back, I put my phone down and stared at nothing.

I ruined everything.

Thoughts raced through my mind, making the minutes feel like hours. My body felt numb and limp. I locked myself out. I shut myself down because I couldn't face the reality of what had just happened. I didn't want to face it. I wished and prayed it was all a nightmare and I would wake up in the trailer again.

But no. It was real. Every. Single. Thing. Happened.

~ • ~

The year that followed passed in a blur. I went on coke benders for weeks at a time. I "ran away" in a Xanax-induced rage. Every time, my dad would rescue me—even though I treated him like shit. He would come and pick me up, and I would have no recollection of the car ride home.

One day he asked me to take the dog out for a walk. It was already afternoon, so this request seemed odd. I could tell he was up to something. I just didn't know what.

"Okay, I'll do it in a second! Let me just get some pants on!" I yelled down the hallway. I closed my bedroom door again and grabbed my black pajama pants with white and dark green lines, the same pants I had worn the day before, and the day before that, and the day before that, and the day before that.

I slipped on my sandals and grabbed Weeaboo's leash. It was a sunny day with a slight cool breeze, the perfect weather. It was hot enough to feel the soothing warmth of the sun, but cold enough to not overheat and get sweaty. Once we came closer to Pine Ridge Park, I pulled a cigarette out of my hoodie pocket and checked my pockets for a lighter.

Fuck, I forgot it at home.

Pissed off, I put the cigarette right back into my pocket and continued with the walk. Weeaboo did his business and we turned around.

I hope my dad goes out at some point today. I really need this cigarette.

He didn't want me to smoke. He didn't want me to do any of it.

I had just come down from a cocaine and acid bender that lasted more than a week, and I needed something to cool my nerves. As I approached my house, I looked up and saw my dad through my bedroom window. I sped up my pace and practically ran to the front door, kicked off my sandals, and ran up the stairs just as my dad left the hallway. The door to my room was wide open. Drawers from my dresser were on the floor, and every single thing that had been on my bed was on the floor. My desk drawers were fully open. I turned around to look into my dad's room and saw all my paraphernalia—my bong, my bag of weed, two grinders, pipes, three empty bottles of alcohol, and a lot of cigarette cartons—sitting on his desk just staring back at me, telling me how badly I had fucked up.

That's it. I'm done. I can't do this. I can't fucking do this! What is wrong with him?! I'm DONE! I CAN'T BE HERE ANYMORE! I CAN'T BE HERE ANY LONGER! I CAN'T DO THIS ANYMORE!

Turning back to my dad, I could feel my heart pounding faster and faster, my head getting hotter and hotter, my eyes getting wider and wider with rage. My vision blurred as my eyes filled with tears.

I return to self-hatred.

Why are you crying? Because you got caught?! Boo-hoo! You're pathetic! This is what breaks you?! Getting caught with all your drugs? You're so disgusting!

Why am I crying, though?

I started punching my wall, letting the rage slowly fuel the pit in me. When I punched harder, my dad yelled, "Olive! Stop punching the fucking walls like a toddler!" But before I stopped, I gave it one last good hit. I stormed out to the back patio and texted my drug counselor, Cassie, in a panic.

Please send me away. I need to leave. I can't be here anymore! Please get me out of here! I don't care where I go! I wanna leave!

While waiting for her response, I texted my therapist, Kimberly, hoping she would respond faster.

Please, someone answer me! I can't be here!

A few minutes later a text appeared from Cassie:

> Hey Olive, I'm so very sorry to hear this. Do you want to call or Zoom?

I typed "zoom," hit send, and waited for the link.

I joined the call and started telling Cassie about what had happened, that I was either going to hurt myself or maybe hurt my dad, that I wasn't safe to be at home, that I needed to leave.

"I'm very sorry to hear that you're having these thoughts and that your dad did all that. Now, I can't really do anything myself unless you want me to send you to a rehabilitation center," she explained.

No, no no, NO! I'm not going to rehab! I'm not that bad!

"I—I don't know what I want you to do, I just texted you in a panic. I just don't know what to do. I just know I can't be here," I cried.

"Well, I can give Kimberly a call and see if she answers," she suggested.

I nodded my head while wiping tears from my eyes. I could hear the ringing from her phone even with the sound of the birds, squirrels, and neighbors around me. I heard a faint female voice answer on Cassie's phone, then Cassie explaining to Kimberly what just happened.

Soon I was on a doxy.me call with Kimberly, who eventually asked to see my room. I went back and flipped the camera to show the tornado that had passed through.

"Holy shit, Olive!" she yelled through the speaker.

I started crying harder. I turned around to face my dad's room to show her all of what my dad found.

"Olive . . ." she sighed.

"Yeah, it's bad. It's really bad. I—I just need to get out of here. I can't be in this house any longer! I'm serious this time, like I really can't be here any longer. If I stay, I know I will go get drugs, then hurt myself, and I really don't want it to be bad. I know it will be. Please send me to the psych ward or something. I just can't be in this house anymore!"

My voice rose with each sentence, each word, each syllable, slowly releasing the pain and guilt of being so low.

"Okay, I will. Now how long can you wait till we can put you in a bed?" she asked.

"I don't know. I just wanna leave as soon as I can. I'm scared of what will happen if I stay for long."

I really didn't care where I went, I just wanted to be somewhere away from him. Soon I went to go pack my bags in the disaster zone that was my room, and my dad drove me to Swedish. We went to the emergency entrance. After twenty other patients, we finally got to the desk. The nurse asked for my name, birthday, and why I was there.

"Are you on any drugs, or have you taken any recently?"

"Um, yeah. Cocaine, DMT, shrooms, Molly, acid, and weed."

Without hesitating, she calmly answered, "Okay, well, we're gonna give you this cup here and I'm gonna have you go into the bathroom and give us a urine sample for a drug test."

I returned with the cup and handed it back to her.

"Alrighty, thank you. Let me just put the test strip in." After a few minutes, she said, "Only weed is popping up as positive."

Shit, I just ratted myself out for no reason.

"I guess it's been enough time for them to leave my system," I said.

"Well, it's time to go into the suicide watch unit. Do you have your things?" she asked.

"Ah, yeah, I do."

"Great. Follow me."

My dad and I followed her away from the receptionist table and through double doors. She turned a corner and led us to a room with glass walls and other patients. The rooms had a glass front wall, and the back walls had a steel garage door, which made the rooms freezing cold.

My father sat with me until we both grew sleepy.

"Alrighty, I can tell that we're both getting tired, so I should get going soon so you can sleep."

No, please don't leave. Please.

"Okay. Will you be here in the morning?" I asked with fear in my voice.

"Don't worry, I'll be here. Just get a good night's rest. You're gonna have a big day tomorrow."

"Alright. I love you, dad. I'm sorry I did all of this, everything I did. I'm sorry. I don't know what brought me here. I'm just . . . sorry."

"Don't apologize. It's okay. You're really strong for doing this, okay? I love you so much," he said. "Goodnight."

He hugged me and left the room.

I wouldn't see him again until the next day, when he would be there to watch me being taken away on a stretcher to the psych ward at Mary Bridge.

That's it. I'm alone. Just me, these walls, and this nurse.

A NOTE FROM OLIVE

Thank you for reading *parts* of my story. There is certainly so much more involved in how I got to my lowest point, but I'm more than proud of overcoming all of that and getting to share my life. Since the last scene of my story, my relationship with my dad has become strong, and we have grown much closer. We trust each other now; we are no longer at each other's necks, waiting for the other to attack. I've hit three years and a month clean from Xanax and two years and seven months clean from cocaine, and I wouldn't be here if my dad didn't do what he did when he did it. My dad is fully the reason I'm sober; he's the reason I'm even alive. I wanted to share my story because I know more and more kids my age who are getting into bad drug addictions and not making it out. I don't want to see another kid's picture flooding my feed on social media unless it's their birthday. Thank you again for reading my story and being a reason why I'm sober today.

OPPOSITE
Jesus Ruiz, Untitled

I PROMISE I'M TELLING THE TRUTH

J McGrath

i don't wanna die
i don't wanna die
i don't wanna die
i don't wanna die

i just don't have an option.

Day 0

Attempting suicide two days in a row scared my doctor a lot, so when my mom asked what to do, my doctor sent us to the Seattle Children's emergency room.

"We can help you here. We can teach you coping skills and help you learn how to deal with your problems," said the intake woman. Her hair—on the lighter shade of brown, the medium length, the way it was kind of curly, kind of not—reminded me of my younger sibling. It was like they'd come as their future self to tell me to get help, to survive, even though they were just waiting for me at home. It made it all the easier to say "yes" without thinking, without understanding, or even considering what my mom thought of the matter. I couldn't have known anyway, since the intake woman said my mom wasn't allowed in the room during the evaluation.

When a bed finally opened up in the Psychiatry and Behavioral Medicine Unit (PBMU) on the sixth floor, someone came to get me from my temporary bed. I sprang up to go, but leg paralysis shot me down onto the floor. The blonde woman who'd come to grab me looked annoyed.

"How long until you can get up?" she asked. She sounded irritated, almost angry.

"Probably a few hours," I admitted, trying to sound confident in myself, but my diagnosis of functional neurological disorder (FND) had only come a month before, so I didn't feel very confident at all. Experiencing paralysis episodes, tics, and difficulty walking had thrown my world upside down, and I had no idea what was coming next. We took the elevator up to the PBMU, and when we got there, they rolled my chair onto a huge scale to weigh me.

She handed me a menu. "This is for all of your food tomorrow. Just circle one of all these, and two of all these," she said, pointing at each section: breakfast, lunch, snack, dinner, and all kinds of sides. When I was done picking, they led my mom and me to the room I'd be staying in for the next week. One of the walls was a stupid bright orange, and it was especially stupid next to the cream on the rest. The window curtains were inside the window, between the panes, as though they were afraid of what would happen if I could see the outdoors unsupervised.

Someone asked if I wanted a snack, and I said yes. That same someone came back with Jell-O and some kind of fruit. The Jell-O was delicious, but it felt like my throat and all of my organs were full of rocks. When they started discussing what things I wanted from home with my mom, and whether I wanted to wear scrubs or my own clothes, I noticed they wouldn't look at me and only spoke to my mom.

I broke.

i can't
stay
i want my mom and dad
this is
exactly
what i asked for
but it feels
wrong
i feel

wrong
but
isn't that
why I'm here?

It was lights-out by the time I showed up, so I had to go right to bed. I slept in the clothes I was already in, and I realized I had no way to know the time. I couldn't even look out the window to estimate. I wasn't allowed to close the door, as I was at risk level three, so the light from the hallway shone into my room like a beacon. Risk levels were based on three categories: how likely you were to hurt yourself, how likely you were to hurt someone else, and your risk of trying to run away. I got zeroes in the violence and run factors, so my level meant that they assumed I was going to try to kill myself.

I don't know when I fell asleep.

Day 1

I woke up to a knock at the door. I opened it to find a man holding a little cup of pills for my anxiety. He stood next to a giant box of a machine.

"I'm here to take your blood pressure, if that's alright with you," he said.

I knew full well that there wasn't an "if" in that equation, that he was only trying to be nice. He put the heart monitor on my finger and the cuff around my arm, and we sat there in silence. I was stunned; I realized I was really here, really going to get help. I took the pills.

I sat around for a while until another man showed up with scrubs and breakfast. After my pancakes, fruit, and egg, I had to get in the wheelchair again. I just sat there, taking in the almost neon wall, when my nervousness kicked in.

What if the other kids don't like me? Maybe they'll think I'm annoying, or too strange.

But once I was led down the hallway and introduced to the other kids in my group, we started making small talk about our names, what group was, and what the food was like.

The day's lead staff member led us down a few hallways to our group room. She handed us our menus and a feelings chart where we recorded how we felt. Pens, pencils, and crayons had all been deemed too dangerous; we could only use markers.

Sometime in the afternoon my mom showed up with a bottle of Snapple peach tea and all my belongings. We had a lot to talk about.

After she left, it was movie time, but we only had thirty or so options. When that time was up, I was taken by some other nurse to the elevator, while my new groupmates took the stairs to the outside area.

It would have been a nice day to lie in the grass, so it was too bad that the only grass was on the other side of the twenty-foot fence. I guessed that they had a lot of people try to, or maybe succeed in, climbing it. The "grass" we did have access to was artificial. It was scratchy and had lots of hair stuck in it. I decided not to deal with that in my chair. I could've gotten up, but I realized my chair was covered in period blood, and the thought of someone seeing that, or even knowing about it, was completely horrifying. So I stayed put.

My dad was in my room when it was time to go back. He gave me wireless earbuds and an MP3 player. It was almost ridiculous how thankful I felt.

After our visit, I wheeled out of my room and asked to take a shower. A staff member unlocked the bathroom door for me. I saw a drain in the middle of the floor and no real designated shower area, despite the short curtain around the showerhead in the corner. I stood up from my chair, using the shower to

wash
the blood
disgusting
horrible
covered in blood
lots and lots
an eternity's worth
of blood

down the drain
never ending
doesn't stop
doesn't know how
to stop
i am no longer sitting
in a growing puddle
of blood
my own
blood
so I'm alright now.

I put on my pajamas, which were all wet from the shower water getting absolutely everywhere. I brushed my teeth and went to my room, and I was careful not to close the door completely. I cuddled up with my dinosaur and attempted to fall asleep to the sound of someone screaming in the hallway.

Day 2

I woke up, and though I couldn't know the time, I knew I woke up early, thanks to the lack of nurses at my door. I asked to go to the bathroom to get dressed, then I went back to my room to put on makeup and do some reading. Turns out I'd gotten blood all over the sheets when I slept. I decided not to tell anyone, and just pretend it wasn't there out of humiliation.

I was attached to the blood pressure machine and given the little paper cup of pills. The nurse asked me if there was anything else I needed.

"Actually, my cane went missing yesterday. Could you look for it?"

"Of course. I'll put a note on your door so people know to look out for it." He pulled out a sticky note, wrote "Missing Cane" on it, and stuck it to the door.

"Thank you," I said.

I know at noon my dad visited and brought me the MP3 player, and at night my mom visited, and no one found my cane. I know we tried to finish our movie, but we couldn't finish it again. I know I got my blood drawn at some point. I followed the required routine, and my parents brought bottles of Snapple for me when they came.

That night, I couldn't get into my room; the wing my room was in was closed off because someone was screaming and hitting people. When I was finally allowed into my room, my mom told me that they had to shut her in it because of the situation. It bothered me to think of her in the same predicament as us patients.

After my mom left, I took a shower and put on my pajamas, but when I opened the bathroom door and took a couple steps back to my room, a kid I didn't recognize ran at me, silently, hands out, trying to scratch me. A nurse told me to run back into the bathroom, and they locked the door behind me. I just

stared
vacantly
this
can't be right
this
is the stuff of movies
real people
real patients
aren't locked in bathrooms
don't attack each other
but i suppose
movies have to have basis
in something.

When they let me out, I went straight to bed. There was screaming again. This time, somebody shut my door. I felt thankful, but the fact that they were so worried made me afraid.

Day 3?

Everything was the same as always. Same blood pressure machine, same blood on the sheets. I practically bled on everything on purpose at this point because I was angry. I had been promised solutions, but so far there had been absolutely none given. I started losing track of time.

A staff member told me they had my cane and that I couldn't have it back. They said I could be a danger, then changed their mind halfway through that thought, and instead said that somebody could grab it from me and hit people with it.

But the damage was already done.

They think of me as a threat, a monster.

I felt grotesque.

The day was dull, monotone, but at one point three of the kids in group decided to run out of the room during free time. They burst out the door and into the hallway with staff chasing them as we

cheer
clap
yell our hurrahs
wave our encouragements
we
are not so brave
yet
we are one collective
one hivemind
they and us
those of us who stayed
share in their glory
their light
their love
their freedom
we share in their
soft air.

As we all knew would happen, once they finally couldn't run anymore, they were put in seclusion. None of them would be back until tomorrow, longer if they didn't fill out worksheets saying they'd never do it again.

My parents both showed up, telling me that they'd had a meeting with somebody. Somebody important, I'd bet. Apparently, someone in charge had said that kids with FND are liars and should be treated as such. I would've been angry if I had any fight left in me.

At some point we all went to bed, and I stared at the light and thought about

glory and
light and
love and
freedom and
soft air.

Day ???
The runners were back when I got to group in the morning, which made me feel good. I'd been worried.

At outside time, some of us sat in the artificial grass talking and picking hair out of it, while others were shooting hoops. My legs went out though, as they so often did. I told our group leader, even though he had scolded us just a minute earlier for saying he looked like his name was Ben. It was immensely disrespectful, and we should never say anything like that to anyone, ever.

After the guy that looked like Ben finished the strangest lecture I had ever heard, I had to tell him, "I can't move my legs. Can you ask someone to bring my wheelchair?"

"I wasn't told you had this problem," he said. He looked and sounded like he'd rather get hit by a truck than be here with any of us.

"Yeah, this happens sometimes."

A pause.

"Well, either I can have someone take you to seclusion, or I can call backup."

Another pause.

"Call backup," I sighed.

"Not Ben" got on his radio and called for someone while I sat there. I couldn't get inside without the wheelchair, so I assumed someone would bring it outside.

Since no patient could be left alone for even a moment, he and everyone else had to stay outside until the person he called showed up. "Not Ben" seemed even more angry at me, and I wanted to cry.

Why is he acting like I want this?

When backup came in the form of a young woman, he wasted no time and left with the rest of my group. Another group replaced us outside, and the woman who was supposed to deal with me also left.

I felt discouraged; she'd looked so nice. She'd had a friendly face and a hair clip with

a bee
on it.
i can't believe
she would just
leave me
here
outside
locked doors to get in
even without locks
i would have to drag myself
against concrete
i am
imploding
my insides curling up
inside of themselves
shriveling up
wearing away
decaying
dying
and i
cry
hard.

After a while I could move my legs, so I stood up and waited for her to come back.

"I can move my legs now," I told her.

She smiled at me. "Perfect. Let's go."

I was humiliated enough to wish that someone would just

end me, so that my neurological disability wouldn't make me feel so guilty and horrible. We went to the group room where the other kids had been sitting around a table together, plotting a way to come get me, to break the rules and help me inside. They all seemed so relieved to see me. I couldn't believe how much they cared.

The Days Blur

I can't remember the exact sequence, but the following events all happened over the course of three days:

—Therapists would show up throughout the day to pull us away, ask if we were depressed, and even if we said no or mentioned we had different problems, they'd still pronounce us "depressed" anyway. I guess that and anxiety were the only problems they knew how to deal with.

The therapist who came to grab me that day took me to a room with unorganized boxes of games, a colorful rug, and a chair. We both sat on the floor and talked about practically nothing. Not long after we'd sat down, my body gave out on me, meaning I couldn't move anything beside my face, so I slumped to my side. The side of my head previously facing away from the wall was now against the wall, because my head was upside down—I had hit the wall and then slid down it in an ugly, contorted position. My side was in complete agony; I felt like my skin would tear if my body slumped any further. Blood started to pool in my head and I wanted to cry. All I could think about was the pain, and the shame of this happening in the first place.

"It's time to go," she said, as if I could do anything with that command. Like everyone else, she'd been told to act as if I were a liar.

"I know."

"We'll leave whenever you feel ready to get up."

I
Lost
It
and
screamed,
"i would, if i could move!"

She seemed entirely unfazed, like she'd expected this response, like it didn't bother her at all. I felt like sobbing and wailing and screeching. But if I did any of that, I would be kept longer, so I kept my mouth shut. After a little bit, I could move again, so I got up and stretched.

"See? That was only fifteen, twenty minutes," she said in a voice so condescending and sickeningly sweet it made me want to puke. I fantasized about hitting and kicking and shrieking at her as much as I could. But of course, I knew better. So I just walked back to group.

—It was dinnertime, and we got to use the dining room, which was usually like a little field trip, but I couldn't move my legs. I stayed sitting on the floor and waited for my wheelchair. After a few minutes, I realized it wasn't coming, and the idea was that I would "stop acting up." Since that's not how anything works, the only thing I could do was

drag
myself
across the floor
like a wounded animal.
palms flat
pulling me forward
i can feel
all
of the dirt
the grime

the filth
the disease
these floors feel
unwashed
unsterile
my hands
are made unclean
the other kids
the whole handful
they follow my lead
and get on the floor
palms flat
sliding
in solidarity
they're exhausted
i'm asked how i do it
i tell the truth
"i have to
i don't have another choice."

I was completely spent by the end of the hallway, once we got to the dining room. I used my arms to lift myself up to my seat. I almost cried out in pain doing it, but I did it, and I ate my mac and cheese with my groupmates. When dinner was over, I asked people not to drag themselves again. I didn't want to get in trouble.

—We had rules in group, patient-made rules that everyone tried their best to follow, always. One of these rules was no yelling. It was lunch, maybe dinner, and a few of us were talking. Apparently too loudly, because our group leader yelled at us to put our plates away. When one person started panicking, something we all knew would happen, we reminded our leader that yelling was not allowed.

"Well, I need to yell if there's an emergency."

"Putting dishes in the cart isn't an emergency."

After some more arguing, she got on her radio and called backup. The backup reminded us, using nicer words, that we were all crazy, so we had to be the wrong ones.

—I didn't know if it was night or morning, but someone was screaming. Just like always. I looked in the plastic mirror in my room, just staring at myself. Before I could really stop myself,

i
scream
too.
i claw
i scratch
i mark
at my arms
my hands
my face
i can't stop
screaming and
scratching
my lungs are out of air
my arms and cheeks are marked
you can see the scratches
my forehead has
tiny
little
red
spots that bleed if you squeeze them
no one comes.

I don't know if staff noticed my scratches. I feel like they must have, but the only people who said anything were my groupmates.

—I was on the floor with leg paralysis for what felt like the hundredth time. This time, though, when I scooted around, I left a trail of blood on the floor. I was completely mortified, but I was in a hospital, so I assumed they wouldn't just leave me to sit in a puddle of my own bodily fluids. After all, everything needed to be clean and sterile. But I suppose cleanliness got in the way of punishment, because all the staff member in charge had to say was, "I'm sure somebody will clean that up."

i feel
disgusting
repulsive
stained
rotten
decayed
unclean.

—A quote from an angry staff member: "If you don't stop messing around, I'm going to pick you up out of your wheelchair, put you in a regular chair, and take your wheelchair away." I didn't move around much after that.

Last Day

Wednesday, my last day. I had saved my nicest outfit just for this occasion: a shirt with a TV quote, a pretty skirt, ruffled socks with little plastic buttons, and ballet flats that were falling apart. I went to group and waited giddily.

Sometime in the afternoon, my mom showed up to group and told me it was finally time to go. For reasons I couldn't put my finger on, I was embarrassed that she was seeing me in the group room. I hugged all my groupmates goodbye, and I made sure I had all the notes my friends had given to me. One of them had been gifted to me sneakily so that he could put his phone number and our real names on it. Staff said they didn't want us stalking each other, so if they'd seen our names and numbers, it would've been confiscated.

After talking with staff about coping skills and collecting all my things, including anything I hadn't been allowed to have—my cane and some makeup brushes—my mom and I left together.

Part of me wanted to hold her hand on the way out, but I was in my wheelchair, so I couldn't. And besides, I didn't want her to know I was a little scared. I had this sense that I was going to get in trouble for leaving.

When we got outside, I was overwhelmed by how open the world was. The lack of walls and fences was stunning, almost too much to handle. My mom helped me into the car, then went to return the wheelchair to the lobby. I stared at the houses by the hospital. I'd never seen them before. The grass, the flowers, the trees . . . it was all so beautiful. If I could've walked, I would've gone and touched every plant.

Eventually my mom came back, got in the front seat, and started driving. I'd missed my mom's car. When we got on the freeway, I was astounded by all the cars on the road. I'd sort of forgotten how many there were. Everything seemed so immeasurable, so

infinite.
the sky
is eternal
everything
is so
enormous and boundless and
dazzling
the outside
the real outside
has no locks
no keys
it is
free and
open
to me
to us
to all
it is
bright and
glittering
it is
forever and

always and
infinity and
eternity
it is
glory and
light and
love and
freedom and
soft air
i'd almost forgotten a world
without walls.

A NOTE FROM J

A couple of months after I went home, I had my first flashback. After months of therapy, I was diagnosed with PTSD as a result of my hospital stay. It's been a couple of years, and I still struggle heavily with it. I still have FND, of course, but I don't mind that so much. Everyone thinks disability's the worst thing that can happen to you, when really, I don't think it's all that bad. Disabled misery's simply the abled person's assumption, usually.

I'm on track to graduate high school next year, and I'm going to college for psychology and religious studies—in case being a famous singer doesn't work out. I wrote this story because it seems like nobody really knows what happens in these types of places, and my story is not at all unique. I didn't even write down everything that happened to me in Seattle Children's. In so many cases, getting help turns out to be more of a punishment than anything else, and this is my way of telling the world how things really are.

This is my movement.

OPPOSITE
Jesus Ruiz, Untitled

MY *TRANS*FORMATION

Rory Gilbert

White walls surround me as I wait in a large maroon chair in the hallway, an overflow for the full waiting area. A large painting of a forest is hanging above me, and I notice that it is perfectly in place—not even slightly askew—as if it was made to be placed on that wall, in that spot.

How can a painting be everything I want to be: someone made to fit, made to belong?

Anxiety crawls into my chest, squeezing my lungs. My Covid mask doesn't make it any better. My leg bounces involuntarily, and my hand clutches the clipboard tightly, my knuckles almost turning white with the force.

I can make out words on the paper below, but my brain can't focus enough to read them. There are boxes I need to mark to confirm that I'm aware of the possible side effects of the procedure: hair loss, heart problems, death.

The smell of bleach, the beep of machines, and the torrential flow of cool air through the vents create a symphony of sensory chords that make me want to get up and run away.

Am I doing the right thing? How many people will I drive away because of this?

The large chair I'm occupying is clearly not made to be where it is. It's placed in the middle of a corner between the hallway and the waiting area, jutting out in the small space. As soon as I feel my heart steadying, a nurse passes with a vitals machine. I curl myself up—tucking my legs in as far as they can go—so that he can pass. His seafoam green mask matches his scrubs, and I can tell he is smiling at me as he passes.

"Thank you," he says kindly and continues pushing his machine down the hall. His smile puts me somewhat at ease until I hear light footsteps from the other end of the hall. A small woman with long, black hair wearing a white lab coat over scrubs approaches me.

"Are you Rory?"

I jump a bit, nod, and get up.

"Yeah that's me," I say as I awkwardly point down to the clipboard.

"Awesome. I'll have you follow me over to the room." She smiles and starts walking to the end of the hall. I quickly follow behind her, trying to calm my heartbeat again.

This is it. I'm so close!

She stops and beckons me into a room, then slides the door shut. She sits down at her desk and gestures for me to sit in the uncomfortable plastic chair beside her. She looks straight at me with tired eyes, but she musters a chipper voice.

"Hello, I'm Adrien, and I'll be the nurse helping you today. Have you ever given yourself a shot before?"

"No." I can feel my hands start to fidget.

"Do you have any experience with needles?"

"Not really, no," I say with an awkward smile hidden by my mask.

After she finishes her sheet of questions, she gets up from her desk, walks over to a cabinet, and returns carrying a tray with two needles, a syringe, a vial of water, some alcohol wipes, and what looks like a piece of squishy fabric.

"This is a fake muscle you're going to practice on."

I can feel my eyes widening at the square of fake flesh. Everything suddenly feels so real. She smiles, seeming not to notice my internal conflict as she walks me through the steps to give myself my first shot of testosterone. As I look at the huge needles, the syringe, and the adhesive bandages on the tray, I'm imagining Adrian cutting off my limbs one by one as I lie back on a surgical steel table like in the film *American Mary*. Or I'm pinned in place by slides of my different body parts lined up in a row—slides showing everything from my blood to the bones in my fingers, like in *Hannibal.*

I can't do anything. I'm frozen in surreal disbelief that my body is finally getting the chance to catch up with my mind. A disconnect I've been aware of since kindergarten and have had to push down until I couldn't push down anymore.

~ • ~

As my new kindergarten teacher's firm hand grasped my shoulder to guide me toward her classroom, my backpack thumped after every step. Before entering, I took a deep breath in the icy quiet, feeling it all the way down in my lungs before taking the last step into the loud room.

Everyone's eyes turned toward me as if I were an albino crocodile balancing books on its tail. The new kid, coming two weeks late into the school year and an hour late to school. In a moment, their loud voices went back to reverberating in the small room. Though not as cold in the classroom, I could still feel the chill in the air. It pinched my arms and caused goosebumps through my shiny blue rain jacket.

My teacher guided me over to some desks, her hand still on my shoulder. She reminded me of a character on Jersey Shore, not quite as loud but still out there in an unpleasant way. She was a tall, blonde woman with her hair cut like jagged shards of glass. She wore wedged high-heeled sandals and blue jeans with bedazzled beads on the pockets. Her perfume stung my eyes.

The class was split into two groups, sitting on opposite sides of the room.

"It's boys on one side and girls on the other. Each group is making something different," she said. Her words stung as I felt my hair rising and a pit forming in my stomach. I begrudgingly took a seat on the girls' side and let my backpack fall to the ground next to me.

I don't want to be here. I don't want to do this. I want to go home.

~ • ~

Over the years, this same scene repeated over and over like a play in purgatory—the default for many school group activities.

In my seventh-grade social studies class, once again, girls sat on one end of the classroom and boys on the other. I was the only one who remained seated in the middle. I felt like I was bracing for war—a war I was all too familiar with fighting. My eyes flashed from one side to the other, expecting an attack from any angle. The harsh whispers scratched my skin. But this time, I couldn't force myself to do it like I always had before. I couldn't force myself to play my required role.

Tears pricked in the corners of my eyes, but I held strong and tried to keep my eyes level. Each group was doing the assignment, but I could tell my teacher, Mr. Bell, was concerned. His eyes also darted back and forth between the two groups, then to me. I watched in mild horror as he picked up the black rotary phone on his desk and spoke to someone in a hushed whisper.

I'm in trouble.

I heard the soft click of the phone as he set it down. He stood at the front of the room and directed the groups to do something else. I couldn't focus, knowing something was coming. Moments later I heard heels clicking in the hall, accompanied by the sound of discussion. There was a light knock, and the door opened slightly to reveal Mrs. Brazil, my homeroom and math teacher, a stern but kind woman. She had high cheekbones and dark brown eyes, and mid length, dark brown hair she kept up in a tight ponytail. Behind her, I spotted Mr. Man, the special education teacher. I didn't know him well, but I knew that he was funny and that he cared deeply about his students; he helped my friend with OCD.

Mrs. Brazil gestured toward me from the slightly open door, prompting me to get up out of the temporary shield my desk provided. I got up slowly, trying to make as little sound as possible, holding onto the pipe dream that people weren't staring with curiosity.

As I made my way over to Mrs. Brazil, I remembered a time when she had spotted me in the hallway, pressed against the wall and just trying to breathe. A large group of kids had passed me, and I couldn't escape the crowd. I hadn't been able to re-create my imaginary bubble—the technique I had learned to manage my anxiety.

"What's wrong?" she asked. "How can I help you?" But I couldn't find the words to reply at the time; I just continued hyperventilating. She held me in her arms and told me to breathe with her.

Since she was aware of the panic attacks I suffered, I knew she had spotted my symptoms: rough breathing, fidgeting, and rubbing away the tears in my eyes.

Outside the classroom door, I was face-to-face with both teachers. Mrs. Brazil spoke first.

"What's going on? Are you okay?"

I could only shrug.

"I've noticed that you've been writing your name as 'Reed' on your papers. Are you trans or gender nonconforming?"

This was not language I was used to hearing. I had found the terms online, so I knew what they meant, but they had never been used to describe me. I wanted to identify as nonbinary, but no one in my family even knew what that meant. It was a word not quite made to fit, like a sweater two sizes too big.

I was so happy to be asked this question that mountains of words were stumbling over themselves to be let out first.

"I don't fit in. I don't feel like a girl. I've never felt like a girl. I can't force myself to pretend anymore. I don't like my chest or my voice. I don't like any part of my body."

The words slipped out of my mouth so fast my mind could barely register them. My breath still hadn't quite caught up with my body, which was shaking uncontrollably. Mrs. Brazil's eyes widened, and her lips moved on words that would not escape. It took a few long seconds for her face to return to normal, and then a small smile peeked through.

"You're the first student to come out as trans at this school. Did you know that?"

I could see her aura warm, and she smiled in an empathetic way I hadn't witnessed before. Then Mr. Man spoke. He had a soft voice—inviting in a way that you felt like you could tell him almost anything.

"Thank you for sharing that," he said. "You know, I feel the same way you do. I feel feminine. I like pink and wearing dresses. I've always felt different from others, but I don't think I could be as brave as you are. My parents weren't the most accepting."

It was so strange; I suddenly felt seen by both people standing in front of me.

I looked at Mr. Man like I was seeing her for the first time, and realized how she always seemed to slouch and hide herself. But at that moment, I saw her stand a bit taller. She transformed before my eyes, and I felt a shift inside myself. I felt like myself for the first time.

~ • ~

Over the next two years, I was admitted to the mental hospital, attended therapy, and started going to a group only for LGBTQ people. After all of that, I decided to go to a school I had heard about, Scriber Lake High School. It was unique, to say the least. Classes were small and teachers were open to different ways of learning. The staff paid attention in a way that those regular schools couldn't. On the flip side, I had also heard that mostly troubled kids attended, those kids who took drugs and got into fights. But I needed a fresh start and Scriber was it.

On my first day of ninth grade, it felt like my second chance at being normal, at blending in. My first class was math. Mike was the math teacher for the whole freshman class. His room glowed with a yellow aura, but that was not what I felt as I sat down at a round wooden table in the back. Dreading roll call, I stared out of the window as people around me chatted softly. It was a large window, one that someone could easily climb out of. I pictured myself climbing out and running past the mote of dry grass into the large row of green speckled trees, then jumping over the fence to be with the squirrels and coyotes. Instead, I sat spinning my pen in my hand as my name was called.

"&*%*," Mike called. It was my dead name. I was expecting it.

I looked around the room, and I spoke at the lowest volume I could manage.

"Actually, I go by Rory."

The room didn't go silent, but I could still feel eyes on me in the supernatural way humans can sense that kind of thing. I kept playing with my pen and looking out the window.

Mike looked up from his clipboard with kind eyes.

"Okay, that's fine with me. Change it with the counselor and you're good to go."

Then he moved down his list. The more names he called, the more students raised their hands, asking to be called a different name.

It was as if I had started a revolution.

I put my pen down and turned my head toward the class. No longer did I have to feel outside; I could be present, with the quiet murmurs and yellow walls, and feel okay.

~ • ~

I feel my brain surfacing back as Adrien continues to explain the process. She moves her lab coat out of the way and sits down at her desk. A clipboard of paperwork sits on her lap.

"Do you want to try practicing on the fake muscle and then giving yourself the shot?"

"Yes," I say, feeling more confident than I have in a long time.

I get up and wash my hands, then dry them and sit back down. Everything in front of me sits in a sealed wrapper on a dark steel tray.

"First you unwrap the larger needle, screw it into the syringe, then pull it back as much as the dosage prescribes," she says. "Then push the air into the vial." She demonstrates the steps as she speaks, then says, "Your turn."

I feel a bit like Dr. Frankenstein injecting a potion into parts of bodies not yet alive. I feel powerful, like I am finally taking my life into my own hands. I am changing myself, all by myself.

Walking out of the office, the confidence I felt holding the syringe fades to numbness as I retreat inside myself; I'm walking and breathing, but not fully there. Stepping into the elevator, I can feel my stomach drop, perfectly in time with the dings of other people stepping off onto their floors.

During the short walk to my car, I try to notice things—how many birds swarm on a french fry, the number of white cars—weird little things to occupy my mind.

When I finally reach my white truck, I can feel my mind chipping away at the block of emotions that sit heavy in my brain. My body is almost on autopilot as I open the rusty door and climb in. The slam of the truck door resets my brain. I look out at the people and other cars ahead of me and start my truck.

It will be a long drive home.

carry it all.

A NOTE FROM RORY

Leaving that appointment, I knew my grandparents would be upset if they knew. They aren't awful people; I just know how they feel about these things . . . changing your body is unnatural in their minds. I love them, but I know that if they found out, our relationship would be nonexistent.

I've been on testosterone for over a year now and I'm feeling better than ever. My grandparents still don't know, and it's for the better. I graduated last year and now go to Edmonds College. My plan is to get a diploma in forensics. If there's anything I've learned, it's that even if the people around you don't support you, there's always someone who will. There are always people who want to see you succeed.

I focus on how happy I feel to finally find confidence. Like I am taking a real step toward a future where I will be happy with my body, a future where I won't hate the reflection that stares back in every store window I pass. My body fits my mind. Maybe my painting is still crooked—still a little off to the side—but not flipped upside down anymore.

I am becoming an adult. I'm ready to do things for myself.

"Pull a smile and wave, nod and look away
wait for it to fade, but it happens all the time
people say it's fine"
—Penelope Scott, "Dead Girls"

REVERSE
Jesus Ruiz, Untitled

FROM FEAR TO FREEDOM: A CONFESSION

Kelsie Beede

I'm sitting in my room full of concert posters and Christmas-colored lights, the only place in the world I feel totally comfortable. As I begin to type this story, I feel vulnerable—like I'm confessing something in front of a large group of people and have to imagine them in their underwear in order to do it. I process things through writing, and I have a lot to process.

Today we learned about conformity bias in psychology class and my mind is spinning. Our teacher, Peter, gave us the definition: "Adapting our behaviors to feel like we belong to a certain group—a deep-seated yearning to feel wanted by the people we choose to surround ourselves with." I'm now filled with questions, doubts, and fears about my life.

I never felt I could be my own person growing up. I was very easily influenced by others—what they did, what they wore, how they presented themselves. I never felt I had the choice to do what I wanted because of my fear of not being liked.

These feelings have been the cause of constant tension, arguments, and countless days when I can't get out of bed. No amount of hair dye, scissors, makeup, or clothes have ever made me feel comfortable in my own skin. I have moments of euphoria after getting new piercings, tattoos, or going to live concerts—or in moments when I can forget my phone is a thing—but eventually I only end up feeling like a re-creation of something I've seen from someone else.

"It's easy to surround ourselves with this behavior, but it's hard to get ourselves out of it," Peter explained as I listened in the dimly lit classroom.

I want to live life. I want to see how beautiful it can be, but I am too wrapped up in how I am being perceived by others.

What happened to the girl I was in second grade? The girl that would only worry about if there was going to be a rainy-day recess? When did I begin to split off from that young, carefree girl?

How can I get myself out of this?

~ • ~

Even though I was nine years old, I still slept in my parents' bed every night because I didn't like the vibe in my own room. One night they thought I was asleep while I was lying next to my mom, facing the wall. I listened as they argued in muffled voices.

"Be quiet, she's gonna wake up," I heard my mom say in an anxious tone.

"She's gonna find out sooner or later," my dad answered curtly, his frustrated energy filling the room.

With that comment, I was fully awake. I had a clue about what was going on. Earlier that day, I was sitting in the living room with my dad as he played *Call of Duty* and watched LiveLeak videos I definitely shouldn't have been watching. His computer was connected to the TV, so all of the violence was playing out in front of me. I never enjoyed these times. I would always ask my mom or dad if I could watch TV, but the answer was always, "Go ask your father" or "I'm busy." When he was done playing, he started scrolling through random files. The ones that popped up on the screen were all his and my mom's personal documents. One that caught my attention was a file under the name of "divorce.pdf." I don't think he realized that I knew what that meant or even that I saw it, but I didn't want to think about it. I ignored it, until I couldn't.

After listening to them argue for a long time, I finally got the courage to roll over, sit up, and ask, "What's happening? What are you talking about?"

My dad stood over my mom, and she seemed exhausted.

Both of them looked at me, stunned, and neither of them spoke. They just looked at each other with a "we're caught" expression.

"Kelsie, your dad and I are getting a divorce."

My body got hot. I felt lightheaded and frayed. Screams started spewing out of my mouth as the tears poured down. I couldn't look at them.

I've always heard them say "I love you" to each other, but was it ever real love?

A few months later I was standing in his girlfriend's kitchen, absorbing everything about the foreign room—the reddish orange tiles and the fridge covered with scattered word magnets. My dad had started taking me on "visits" there. Even though he was still living at home, I knew he was staying there sometimes.

I noticed a black-and-white photo hidden by the magnets. A baby.

Who is it? Not her son . . . the date is recent.

I don't know how long I was standing there, staring into space, when I heard my dad yell, "Kelsie, let's go!" from down the hall. I decided to put the picture in the back of my mind. I ran out the door.

A few weeks later, at my house, I heard my parents fighting in their bedroom. Only this time it felt a lot more serious.

"Get out now!" my mom screamed, fear and pain coating her words.

My grandma and I were in the living room sitting on the couch. I looked at her with concern, but her gray bangs covered most of her expressions; I couldn't see her reaction.

My mom came out of the bedroom and stomped toward me.

"Guess what?! You're going to have a new sister!"

I thought my mom got her tubes tied? Why is she upset about it?

It finally hit me later that night what she meant.

~ • ~

The deep yearning to feel wanted has defined so much of my life. I begin untangling knots regarding the anger I feel when I think about my dad deciding to leave fifteen years of marriage and his three kids behind with my mom, dumping so much heartbreak on her.

And I can't help but feel jealous every time I see my little sisters—his two daughters from his second marriage—play with him. When he chases them around or throws them in the air, and they laugh and scream and show their big toothless smiles to the world, I feel nauseous. All I can do is try to find a distraction from the resentment building inside of me. The truth is that I would do anything to be in their place and get a moment like that with him.

I love them, and they love me. Ages five and seven, they both make it clear they want to be like me when they grow up. They want my red hair and piercings, and they are always begging for my attention. I am happy they have grown up feeling secure, with parents who aren't struggling with money and who care about them.

I want to be happy for them. And I don't want to make their happy moments about myself. But they both look like me—we share the same huge eyes and similar facial features—so it is a challenge not to make it about myself.

I don't remember him being around when I was that age. Until recently, I had no memory of laughing and playing with him.

~ • ~

My mom came into my room and handed me a camcorder. "I found this in storage collecting dust. Do me a favor and look through this real quick," she said, then left.

One of the first things I found was a video of me when I was around six years old. I hesitated. I was nervous to watch it, and kind of frozen. I saw the still shot of me, and I knew who was filming it because of the high angle. I finally pressed "play" and listened to my young voice take over the silence in the room.

"I go into grandma's room to get this," my young voice says, holding a statue of an angel.

Then my dad's booming voice breaks in. "Hey, Kelsie . . . Kelsie . . . I love you," he says.

My face looks straight at the camera, and with a huge grin, I say, "I wuv you!"

I smiled at my voice, but I was holding back tears. My body felt light, like I was floating. My heart felt full and free seeing myself having fun with him, but my stomach felt empty—slightly uncomfortable and queasy, like it wasn't even me in the recording. I looked so different.

I played it over ten times. Each time, the pressure behind my eyes built until it felt like a dam about to break.

When my mom came back into the room, I tried to hide my emotions. I didn't want her to feel bad for showing me the footage.

"You look so cute!" she said. She didn't say anything about my dad.

I hadn't remembered that moment with him, but there it was.

We continued to look for more footage of me as a child and discovered fond memories with my brother. It was refreshing to see those lighthearted videos, but it was hard to focus on them, because all I could think about was the one with my dad. I desperately wanted to feel that laughter and closeness with him again, but all I could find was a desolate space. The look on my mom's face betrayed her own deep sadness; I knew we were both distracted. I was usually open with her, but I felt that by hiding my emotions, I could protect her.

~ • ~

I take a break from writing this story and leaf through my notebook. I find a poem I wrote and realize the connection between it and what I'm trying to untangle. The poem is about the first time I was trying to figure out what a relationship was. It was the first time I thought something between me and someone else might be real love.

I remember finding out it wasn't actually love.
Looking up I see the old popcorn ceiling that's turning yellow from age and cigarette stains. I am gripping onto my phone and it feels like it should snap any second. I don't smell anything, it's all stale old air. Humid air is everywhere, picking at my red undertone skin. I taste anger, I taste the lies you told me for months, I taste bitterness, I taste blood.
I hear static and faint thumping all around.
I am in my grandma's living room, sitting on her chair in her apartment.
There's a big sliding glass door that overlooks the pool. There's a shelf barricading my view. Sitting on cotton and old memories. I don't think I can really feel my breathing.
I remember finding out it wasn't actually love.

Seeing how my parents' relationship landed, I have feared the same thing would happen to me. With my luck, it did. I recognize the connections from things my mother has told me about her and my dad to little things that happened in my first "relationship," like hearing the words *I love you* followed by a disappearance, leaving me in the dust. It should've never gotten this far—to the point where I never wanted to be vulnerable with anyone again.

After what happened the summer before my ninth-grade orientation, I'm surprised I was able to let anyone in, under any circumstances. I felt completely lost. No one knew what was going on behind closed doors. My family didn't know me. My friends didn't know me. And I certainly didn't know me.

~ • ~

The smell of cheap shampoo and outside air creeped in, invaded my senses, and wrapped around my mind as I slid down the old bathroom door in distress. I brought my hands up to my head, felt around my curly hair, and touched my hands to my lips and up to my eyes, realizing I couldn't feel what I was doing. It was the night before my freshman year orientation at Lynnwood High School, and the only thing I wanted was to be five again.

It hit me that I was growing up, not as a choice but as a punishment. I was a stranger to my own self. I wanted to be free. Everyone was excited to start high school, but I wondered if they thought it was going to be like the movies where everything was perfect. I knew I wouldn't have the experiences I wanted and hoped for. I was already so behind when it came down to other things in life. I never had a boyfriend or girlfriend. I was called "boring" if I didn't want to do something risky but "annoying" or "pushy" when I did want to go out and have some fun.

I felt like this was all tied to not ever getting to be a carefree kid. My dad wasn't really home before the divorce, and mom was too worn out to do anything. After my dad left, my childhood was filled with fear and never knowing if I was going to have a bed to sleep on, or food to eat. I couldn't tell anyone what I was feeling because I was afraid of hearing "I felt the same when I was your age," "you're just overthinking all of this," or "everyone feels like that." Phrases like that—when I felt as though my soul was being ripped out of my body—made me feel desensitized to everything. I felt like nobody listened to me or wanted to hear my truth. I was a shadow. I was everyone else's therapist.

My body absorbed the heat that slowly surrounded the small room. It was hard to breathe. My chest was tightening so much it felt like it was going to explode.

At the age of fifteen, I needed to find a way out of growing up. Anything would be better than having to deal with myself and the unbearable pain in my chest. I settled down on the cold tile of the bathroom floor with the intention of meeting what was on the other side.

I got up after what felt like years and looked in the mirror. The image didn't look like me, and I didn't feel like me. I tried to see the four-year-old that begged my mom to come home from work, or the six-year-old wearing her purple polka-dotted dress with black leggings and boots topped with the huge birthday hat covering the messy blonde hair. It had been my birthday that day, in Mrs. Mason's kindergarten class at Cedar Valley, and my dad had taken the picture. I was smiling. Who doesn't like going to school on their birthday? I got to celebrate with my friends!

Where was that six-year-old's joy?

I told myself exactly what I had to do to seal the deal.

I want it to stop I want it to stop I want it to stop

I closed my eyes as the cold razor blade went into my skin, followed by instant heat seconds after. It went in over and over and over again. Tears soon came pouring down my face from the pain and regret over what I had just done. I couldn't breathe—my lungs felt like they were about to collapse and crush me.

What am I doing? What was I thinking?

I have to get rid of the evidence.

I wrapped up the blade in toilet paper and shoved it in the trash. Putting the adhesive bandages on felt humiliating.

Why did I do that?

The only thing that kept me from following through with it was the family that couldn't seem to function. Not being able to see my siblings grow up and see their full potential. Wondering if I was ever going to find love.

One Year Later

Just weeks away from graduation, I find another poem. I wrote it for an English assignment my junior year. We were supposed to personify objects in our rooms that said things about us. As I read it, I realize how far I've come.

> She's a people watcher, waiting for something interesting to happen, say the open blinds in her room.
> But not a person who doesn't have a dream, say the stacks of poetry books on the side table.
> She likes to feel like she's not always alone, says the TV that is always on no matter what.
> They feel absolutely everything but nothing at all, says the absurd amount of heavy blankets and the overshared thoughts written into dreadful journals.

I can see how, with the help of therapy—having a space where I could freely let my thoughts out to someone who was willing to listen—I was able to change mentally and physically. For two years my therapist, Lindsey, told me to "do it scared." During our last session together, she told me "You are not the same Kelsie I met over Zoom during the pandemic."

Now I am the one who is out, making life interesting. I'm publishing my story and my poetry, and my TV is never on anymore. Instead, the silence in the room is filled with the laughter of the ones I love. I'm no longer hiding under blankets; instead, I'm reaching out to others and exploring my world. I have a boyfriend whom I love and dream about—someone who loves me who isn't family. This is a new version of myself that I never thought would become reality, a me that has dreams. Seeing this person in real life, standing in front of the mirror I once was never able to look at, is all I've ever wanted.

Through the years, one dream that kept me sane and going was the simple hope of making it through to the other side. On my laptop screen an email I just received reads:

> Dear Kelsie,
>
> Welcome to Edmonds College!
>
> Today marks an important milestone in achieving your dreams. You are standing at the starting line of your educational journey, and all of us here are standing alongside you.

I feel tingly. Being at this steady and easy pace feels strange. I enjoy it, though.

I'm about to walk across the stage to receive my diploma. I'm going to college in the fall.

I'm living life. I'm getting closer to having the freedom I crave.

I've untangled so much.

I'm seeing how beautiful it is.

A NOTE FROM KELSIE

Seeing where I came from and what I've been able to do with my life is such a freeing thing to experience. Even though I still fear growing up and what else I might miss out on, I no longer have a stuck mindset. It has really helped to go through therapy and see the world in a whole new light. Believe people when they tell you therapy can change you. I feel like I'm my real age now—more than ever before. I am now responsible for myself and care about my future. Marjie has helped me through most of it and has shown me that my ability to write can impact other people in a way I never realized before; my story can help someone who feels the same as me. I appreciate all the help, even when I was being stubborn and blind to reality.

carry it all.

REVERSE
Jesus Ruiz, Untitled

DRIVE

Madelenn Markfield

I'm a liar. One of the biggest there is. I have lied to everyone—my friends, my family, and even myself. But that's not the most ironic part. I have a genuine thought that plagues my head like a chronic disease: the belief that I never lie. I mean, even at this moment, I find it perplexing, the irony and abstract idea of the phrase "I never lie" being a lie. My head circles on this fact, trying to ground itself in the familiar sights of my classroom's beige desks and the gray carpets that ease my worries.

I'm typing, rather than writing with a pencil. The paper's too thin, and the sound of lead dragging across paper is too loud. The sound of music fills my head instead, my small earbuds vibrating to make sounds into words and meaning. I'm communicating with my fingers at every press of the keys on the keyboard. It's a strange feeling, my thoughts being expressed on a bright screen that I'm surprised isn't hurting my eyes. But regardless, I'm still sitting in my seat, feeling the hard plastic on my bones while I finally tell the truth. The tremor in my hands from anxiety or perhaps my ADHD meds helps to ground the fact that this is real, that my lying is an undeniable truth.

My mind is swimming with possibility at what I've just discovered. A list of lies I've told others and myself. The lies range from positives to just false beliefs and realities: *I'm fine. I can handle it. I'm enough. I'm not sick. It doesn't matter.* I know they're simple, but they have become my world, my reality, and the axis I spin on.

It seems like it's always been this way. The line from "Wolf in Sheep's Clothing" by Set It Off plays—"Telling all your lies like second nature"—confirming my thoughts. As I write, I'm beginning to unravel the lies that knot my head together and tangle my heart in the mix. I'm beginning to understand the tight sinking feeling of my heart in my throat and the static in my head.

I can't really remember when my lying started, but I know that in sixth grade I would obsess over lunch and lie that it was fine, that I was fine.

~ • ~

I sighed, sleep not leaving my fatigued body. The usual dizziness of morning caused disorientation and confusion. I stared at my lunch bag, the gray-lined insides, and the random design on the outside. *Ice pack*, I remembered. *I need to bring an ice pack.* I moved, my body tense as I turned around, blindly reaching for the freezer handle and pulling the door open.

My hand fumbled until it hit the bitter coldness and damp feeling of a bright blue ice pack. It had remnants of a sticker, the paper becoming crumpled and discolored to a dull gray. I placed it in the empty bag while continuing the losing staring contest. My mind was racing with thoughts I couldn't process. *What should I eat? I don't want to eat. You still need to. What should I pack?* These thoughts weighed on my mind like a world on my shoulders. It felt unfair. I didn't know how to pack a lunch, but I couldn't ask. No, I couldn't bother my mom; she was sick with undiagnosed fibromyalgia and had more important things to worry about.

I glanced around, finding the ramen packet quickly. I held it, hesitating and unsure, before I turned around and put it next to the ice pack, forgetting about my plan to pack more. *That should be fine, right? I'm not hungry, and eating will just make me feel sick. I'll eat snacks when I get home. My friends don't eat much anyway.* I justified all these things to myself, only to take another three minutes of processing to be sure.

Lunchtime finally came, my time to eat and pretend I wasn't sick or bored of the repetition of eating. I was surrounded by my friends—all of them thin, healthy, and wanted. I took out my lunch bag and pretended I wasn't on the verge of shaking and crying. I placed it in front of me, opened the bag, and stared for a long moment at the one edible thing in it: the pack of dry ramen noodles. *I'm so hungry. This is what you deserve for being so lazy this morning. You should lay off the food anyway, you eat too much. No one cares anyway.*

I crushed the noodles and opened the packet while I talked to my friends. No one seemed to notice my lack of food; if they did, they didn't say anything.

"Oh, I don't eat a ton, it's okay," I'd lie if they asked, laughing about how I didn't have much food. I ignored the bitter taste of lies and betrayal on my tongue as I thought, *I have plenty of food.*

~ • ~

A new beat echoes in my ears, signaling the beginning of "Karma" by AJR. The lyrics stand out, unwinding another old knot: "I've been so good, but it's still getting harder." It sticks to me, a new bandage attempting to rip my skin off with every pull. It grounds me like the smooth texture of the keyboard and reminds me of how far I've come since the beginning. It reminds me of seventh grade, the lies that became my only truth. The panic attacks consumed me almost as much as the thought that I wasn't enough, that I had to try harder.

~ • ~

Stepping into the counselor's office was both a blessing and a curse. I was relieved to be away from the classroom and free from the expectations and responsibilities of being a gifted student. However, I also felt I was just wasting time. *I knew this was gonna happen. I knew my brain would lie and tell me I'm making excuses, that I'm just attention-seeking.* But still, I sat in the familiar plush chair and tried to find my reasoning, the rationality that maybe I was being genuine.

The gentle smile and soft features of my counselor assured me that it was okay, that I could be okay, that I was telling the truth. That feeling lasted about ten seconds before it came crashing down. "What's wrong?" she asked, using a tone that felt too calm for the chaos raging against my skull.

The anxiety, fear, and worry rushed back, accusing me of lying. My heart was lodged in my throat, and my head was fuzzy, full of static and dull sensations. Each breath was more like a desperate gasp for air, everything so shallow and numb it felt unreal. *Maybe I'm really not breathing.* My eyes blurred and my vision tunneled. I could see the shapes of fidgets and potted plants and the outline of someone sitting in front of me. It suddenly felt like I was watching a movie or playing a game; I wasn't actually in the situation, just watching it play out.

I sighed heavily, then tried to pull some oxygen into my panicked mind. Reaching for a clean tissue, I began to shakily tear it apart, the dust settling and floating around in the air around me. Had I not been looking at the tissue, I would have seen the eyes of concern staring at me. *I'm being really annoying again. How come I can't go to class?* As if on cue, I heard my counselor ask, "Do you need to go home, or can you go to class?"

Those dreaded words gave me options yet made me feel even more trapped. I knew my expression betrayed me; I looked disinterested rather than disappointed. She couldn't understand my thought process, how I felt expected to go to class, even though I was fighting off a panic attack. I didn't look sad or angry, I just looked bored. I didn't know how to express myself, how to tell them what emotions were racing through my head or how the heaviness of my thoughts weighed on my mind. I even doubted whether I was upset.

Loneliness and grief raged in my veins, coursed through my body, and reminded me that no one could understand how I felt. How every ounce of my being just wanted to be okay, to be listened to, and to finally be taken seriously. But if I wanted that, I had to work for it. I had to try harder. They all saw the gifted and responsible exterior, not the decaying insides full of anxiety and doubt. I just needed to try harder and they would see, they would see it wasn't an excuse.

As the dismissal finally set in, my eyes began to tear up. My voice wobbled as I repeated the rant I had been saying all year: "I want to go to class, but I don't think I can. I'm anxious." I sniffled and brought a new tissue to my nose and wiped it. I felt hopeless, lost, abandoned, and so alone. No matter how many times I tried to explain it, they never understood.

I gasped for breath, my mind racing through the possibilities of my options. Sure, I could go home, but that felt like I was just making an excuse. I was expected to stay at school. I was capable of staying at school. So why was it so hard? In the end, I went home. Even though I knew I needed to go, I still felt worse than before. The work wasn't difficult, my teachers were nice, and I even had some friends. But for some stupid reason, I just felt so scared and unsure. I felt weak, embarrassed, and like I was just making it up.

Try harder.

~ • ~

"The Kid I Used to Know" by Arrested Youth starts playing, signaling a new mantra: "I'm not another sick, sad tragedy." The lyric plays over and over, fueling my fingers to type more and more, and flooding my head with water and lies. The lies that sway like ocean currents, the lies that say I'm okay, that I'm not sick, and that I've never been sick. I know the lyrics are a lie. I *am* sick. It's the same type of truth as the ground we walk on, undeniable no matter how hard you want to ignore it.

~ • ~

You don't have enough time to look. The thought circled in my head as the cold water of the bathroom sink hit my trembling fingers. I was already cold, but I didn't bother to warm up. The shivers made the fear and hunger go away. I didn't have to think about anything but my head, and that was good enough. I sighed, glancing up at my masked face and black sweats in the countertop mirror. I didn't know what would happen if I stared for too long, and I wasn't about to risk someone finding out that I wasn't okay.

I had made it to residential eating disorder treatment, just like I had wanted, yet I felt like I was just being dramatic . . . that everyone would find out I was faking it.

I turned around, watching as a staff member began to move down the small hallway and into the foyer before stopping. I took that as my moment to go back to the living room with all the other girls. I plopped down on my seat, feeling a shiver rake through my body. It was proof that I deserved to be there. Proof that I was sick enough to have treatment, that I was enough. To finally prove that I wasn't lying, that I wasn't just making up all my problems.

I stared at the window, watching the rain drizzle, then watched the other girls go about their activities. Some were drawing, others reading, one or two were playing games. I thought about joining them, but the feeling of judgment froze my movements. *They don't want you to play. You don't deserve to be here. You're a liar.* I bit my lip, trying to ground myself and remind myself that it wasn't the truth; they liked me, they wanted me to play. I was sick, too. I rubbed my arms, tempting to dig my nails into my skin and feel some sort of new and controlled sensation.

However, I was too scared to follow through on harming myself and risk people becoming concerned. For them to realize I really do need help, that I'm not just some depressed, unmotivated teen, but someone battling every movement and thought. They wouldn't understand; I was just making it up. Sure, I was in a residential treatment facility, a level of treatment just below psychiatric inpatient, but I didn't feel sick like everyone else. No, they weren't making it up. *I'm just doing this for attention. I'm just doing this to make myself feel better, to prove I am sick, too.* I needed to be like this, I needed to not eat, I needed to be cold. I needed to act like nothing was wrong, because there wasn't anything wrong. *Oh, I'm just not very hungry, I don't eat a lot.* My secret, the secret that no one could know. *I'm not actually sick.*

~ • ~

The new song envelopes me, taking apart my carefully constructed lies and reality. Alec Benjamin's song "Demons" plays: "For a moment I thought maybe I was doing alright." My reality is changing as I type and hit enter on the keyboard. It's an eye-opening process where I know, I actually know, I'm not okay. I haven't been okay.

~ • ~

Being moved to outpatient eating disorder treatment from residential treatment had eased the dullness in my head, allowing my thoughts to be clearer. I understood that I wasn't okay, that I never had been. I couldn't fool myself anymore, not with the sun piercing the curtains or the sound machine buzzing in my ears. This was real. This was reality.

"I don't know what to do. I'm tired of feeling this way," I said, disrupting the silence. I was sitting across from my current therapist. She was one of the few that worked in my outpatient program. She made me feel validated as few had, even though I had a rocky start. Getting out of residential due to insurance was definitely not on the agenda for my mental health.

She stared at me, absorbing and thinking about all the information I shared. She didn't smile, but even if she did, I wouldn't know with the cloth mask covering her face.

"It doesn't change overnight, but that's why you're here," she explained, the words sinking into my chest.

Will I really be able to get better?

~ • ~

The last song rings through my ears, ending my chorus of memories and the reminders of all I've survived. The song "UH OH!" by Sub Urban, featuring BENEE, plays long after I finish the original draft for this story. The single lyric, "Fool me once, that's one too many," reminds me of the first time I admitted my habit of lying. I had thought it was over, that I was finally done lying and faking everything. Yet, exactly one year after my return home from residential treatment, the reality of my biggest lie came rushing toward me like a hurricane. A lie in which I faked my entire existence, the lie that I wanted to get better.

~ • ~

My hand shook as I gripped the blue marker and crossed off my next word. There was little to do in psychiatric inpatient treatment, but I had been passing the time by doing word searches, a mindless activity that took me out of reality. Even with the large, sealed windows and bright, colored walls, everything just felt like a scene in some kids' movie. I wasn't the main character. I didn't need to smile or pretend. I just existed as a background character to fill the space.

The others there, a mix of different genders and ages, were the ones destined to move on, to learn and get better. I was only there to give an example of the pain of reality and truth. I was just there as a reminder to adults that the statistics were real and that I was going to become one of them.

My head was constantly consuming me, time passing in a blur of words and movements, white paper and therapy activities, of lying in a stiff bed with lightweight blankets. I tried not to sink into my head, into that space that a small part of me knew was a lie—the reason I was there in the first place. I had a plan. I had the motivation and desire to end my life, become a statistic, and hope no one would blame me too much.

Yet, there had been a small, extremely fragile part of myself that didn't want that. My mind screamed at itself and my body that this was wrong, that I didn't need to become another sob story. All I had been through constantly cycled through my head: lying about being hungry, lying that I was okay and getting better, lying that I wanted to get better. All I had been through was coming to a stop. A record player that finally reached its end after the continued songs and words. No one was there to reset me, or to reassure me that I could become a new record instead of repeating the same sad story again.

My movements, my words, and even my thoughts weren't mine anymore. Someone—no, something—was controlling my movements, making me watch in third person as time passed. I watched as I walked to the cafeteria every day, as I took my handful of pills every morning, as I laid restlessly in that uncomfortable, unfamiliar bed. Even if I clawed at my wrist, breaking skin and focusing on the sting of nerves touching the air, I couldn't believe it was real anymore.

Dissociation or, in more specific terms, derealization was plaguing my mind like a deadly disease. It didn't matter if I was cold or hot, it didn't matter that the lights were too bright and the noise too loud. The only thing that mattered was the endless cycle of waiting until I had a chance to make it all go away. Plans to hide a spork, plans to clog the drains, plans to do something so it stopped. It hadn't been a cry for help, but instead the truth I hid so carefully.

I don't want to get better.

~ • ~

I'm finishing my writing. My fingers slow on the press of the keys, edging to the end of my story, but not the end of my journey. While my bones still hurt and my hands shake, my head finally feels clear. With the static and dullness of depression and anxiety eased, all the different songs and tunes of my life come together in a jumbled melody. It's chaotic, yet it feels so real, so genuine, and so right. I can't say it's all over, that I'm all better, because I'm not. I'm happier, freer, and more content, but I'll always have new knots to work out. I know I'll never catch up, but I can hope.

Unlike my younger self, I know when I'm lying and trying to escape reality. I recognize the clouded feeling of thoughts lingering around my head and the monochrome glasses through which I viewed everything. While I can't say I'm ever going to have a rose-colored view, my life is still a lot more colorful. I can now take the good and the bad and weave it together into something strong, stubborn, and changing with the times, yet still mendable. I might not be okay now, but I *can* be okay.

I *will* be okay.

A NOTE FROM MADDIE

The whole message of my story and the open ending is to portray a part of mental health that the media often brushes over. Just because someone is getting help does not mean they want help. Which might seem small but is a really big thing. Because, sure, at the beginning of a headline, it talks about how depressed Person A was, how they involuntarily went into treatment, but what do you know, by the end of the article Person A has found the light at the end of the tunnel and is totally fine now. Reality goes a little bit differently. There is no "end" to mental health treatment.

For starters, actual mental illnesses don't go away. While some people experience mental health issues, they don't always experience a mental illness. I don't say this to invalidate, because it has as much to do with severity as it does with duration and brain chemistry. My brain, quite literally, is wired to think negatively. Instead of being excited about ice cream, I worry that I'm going to drop it and make a mess and never enjoy the money I just spent. Why is this important? I struggle with the concept that one day I'm just going to "get better." For example, I could have easily shown that when I got out of psychiatric inpatient, I started to improve drastically and I've felt a million times better since. However, I chose not to. Instead, I left readers with something to think about. It ends right at a critical point of my recovery, where I realize I don't want to get better, but my story continues. I didn't need a happy ending, nor did I need to completely change myself to move forward. I'm learning to be content with life, that everything is temporary, that there isn't an end point I should be looking for. I'm going to be sad, I'm going to be happy, and sometimes I'm just going to be. Learning to accept this has been such an important part of my journey, yet I almost never see this portrayed in real-life media. I just hope both my story and my notes help serve that purpose. As Noam Shpancer, a psychology professor who wrote the novel *The Good Psychologist*, says, "Mental health . . . is not a destination, but a process. It's about how you drive, not where you're going."

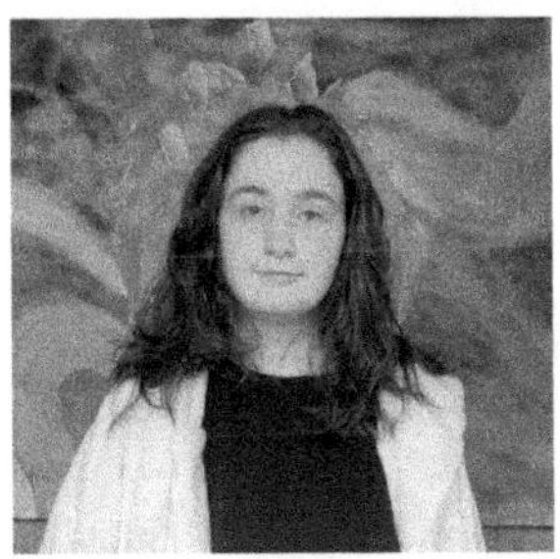

OPPOSITE
Jesus Ruiz, Untitled

LIKE BLACK ON MIDNIGHT TREES

Turtle

I can't remember the details.

Every time I try to recall certain events, a wall of clouds floats into my vision like a ghost, blocking my path—no matter how hard I try to push past or pull it away.

I catch glimpses of when I was a kid, before my parents got on drugs. But I remember very little about anything that happened afterward, when I went to live with my great grandma, except for what other people have told me.

It sucks because I want those memories. I want to be able to remember my childhood, so I can learn from my parents' mistakes and change my life for the better. I know I'm going to be a great person—and a great father to my kids in the future—because I won't make the mistakes my parents did. I know I can learn from my grandma's mistakes, too. I won't be a drinker like her. I won't do drugs like them.

The reason I need to write this story—the reason it's so important—is to remember. I'm piecing everything together, starting with my lowest point, and how I slowly rose from there to the place I am now, reunited with my mom, ready to graduate and move into my future.

~ • ~

After being at school all day, I had just sat down on our old gray couch and picked up my old gold PlayStation controller when my grandma walked into the house carrying groceries. It was Friday, and I knew groceries meant alcohol. I was in ninth grade, and I had just moved in with my grandma after getting kicked out of my great grandma's. I was finally growing up and learning about the world. I thought our new place was cool because I had the biggest room (after the master bedroom).

I walked into the kitchen to check out the groceries. There were still dishes in the sink and dirt hid in all corners of the room. But it was cleaner than usual.

"Man, I'm about to have me a fun night," my grandma said with a sly chuckle, as if she hadn't been getting blackout drunk every night for the past few weeks. She was wearing her usual yoga pants, black jacket, and grayish hair pulled back into a bun. She looked at me and said, "Don't worry, I'm only going to have a shot."

I sighed and picked the Reese's peanut butter cup out of the plastic bag, which was sitting next to the open bottle of Crown.

"You reek," I said under my breath.

"What did you say to me, boy?" she asked, almost screaming in my ear.

"Nothing, Grandma."

When I finished my Reese's, I walked back over to the couch and sat down on the rough surface, the soft pillows somehow caressing me without being the slightest bit comfortable. I pressed the button to turn my controller on and loaded up a game I had been waiting all day to download—*Ghost Recon*. I was so excited to play I could barely contain myself. After learning the game and gaining levels for about an hour, my grandma stumbled out of the kitchen and gave me a look of disgust mixed with disinterest.

"What are you doin', faggot?" she said as she stumbled into the room. "Faggot" was the name she called me when she was "just playing." She only said things like this when she was drunk.

I answered in a calm, sweet voice; I was used to this. I knew better than to start something with her in this state.

"Nothing, Grandma. What do you want?"

"What do you think you're doing, bitch? Stupid bitch. I'm gonna kill you, you stupid bitch!" She was trying to keep her balance and keep her drink from spilling over as she yelled at me.

I paused *Ghost Recon* for one second to stop myself from dying midgame. I looked up at her and lost volume control.

"What are you even talking about right now?" I yelled. I stopped paying attention to her for just a moment, and she pounced on me from behind.

"Why are you always on that Game Boy?" she screamed, stumbling over to my PlayStation, cords still attached to the TV on the wall and connected to the Wi-Fi box. She reached up, grabbed the cords, and ripped the whole thing up off the floor, waving it around like she was going to smash it.

I stood up and screamed, "Get your hands off my fucking shit!"

I reached my hand out and grabbed the PlayStation, twisting to put myself in front of her when the unthinkable happened: she fell over.

Suddenly she was on the floor, drunk and pissed off, screaming her head off about me hitting her when I never laid a finger on her. Adrenaline took over and I rushed to my room with all my stuff, trying to hide from all the thoughts in my head.

"Worthless faggot! Dumb bitch! You're wrong . . . all of you is wrong!" she yelled after me.

But instead of me just hearing the words this time, my grandma was so loud that the neighbors could hear, too.

A few days later my grandma threw a party for our whole family. She always thought she was doing everyone a favor by getting us together, but it never turned out well. When my uncle showed up, I realized that he wasn't there for the party—she had asked him to come to deal with me over the "hitting" incident.

I was sitting on my bed in my room after everyone went to the store, trying to stay calm. I knew it was only a matter of time before someone came after me for the thing I didn't do. Suddenly, the door burst open and clanged against the wall. My uncle came barreling through like a bull with a thick black belt in his hand.

Alright, let's just get this over with.

But he didn't want to hear anything from me. He just started laying into me with the belt, making it crack against my skin. *Wack, wack, wack, wack.* He got eight hits in before I could even ask why.

I stared at him as he hit me, holding in my screams so he wouldn't get any satisfaction. Finally, I screamed, "Okay, okay, stop, dude!"

The pain must have been so clear in my voice that he looked almost shocked when he heard it. But then he gripped my head in his hands and yanked it two inches from his face.

"If you ever do that again, I will kill you," he said. He shoved my head away, then turned and headed out the door while I stifled tears and screams.

When everyone returned, my whole arm was so black and purple and swollen that everyone thought it was broken.

~ • ~

After my uncle beat me up, all I did was disappear. I wanted to play video games, sleep, and get high. At the end of my freshman year, the pandemic hit and everything shut down. All classes were on video, so that allowed me to do exactly what I wanted to do: sleep and sleep and sleep some more. It allowed me to do whatever I wanted without consequence. My grandma stopped trying to control things. We just . . . coexisted.

Every day I would lay on my soft, single bed—my feet hanging off the end because it didn't fit me anymore—pull my soft fleece blanket over my head, and struggle to keep my eyes open. My arms felt like a thousand pounds as I would grasp onto my Chromebook and pull it close to me.

"Go back to sleep," a voice would whisper every morning, nudging me back into oblivion.

"Sleep, Boy, sleep. You're gonna need it for tomorrow when you sleep some more," it would whisper more and more loudly, my ears growing warmer.

My eyelids would droop even lower as I was admitted into Zoom class. The screen would flash white and suddenly my eyes would be open again, as if I was dreaming about watching the screen.

"Hey everyone, hey teacher," I would say in greeting, my audio on and my camera off. Then suddenly I would be out, drifting back into deep slumber, never to be disturbed again.

Yet I never got enough sleep.

I slept through the rest of my ninth-grade year, trying to make sense of all the things going on around me. When the pandemic continued into the next year, all I did was sleep more and more. That was the only thing that made sense to me.

~ • ~

Junior year was back in person. I was relieved to finally interact with people again, not just sitting in my room wasting away like an overgrown vine. I still struggled to wake up every day, and depression stuck to me like black on midnight trees.

One day toward the end of the year, the sun was hiding behind dark, angry clouds. The soft pitter-patter of rain splashed around me while I slowly walked up the 126 old stone stairs to school. My bag felt heavy on my shoulders, the weight pulling me down. The loud sounds of drums and autotune played from the Juice Wrld song in my old headphones as my beanie slipped down over my eyebrows.

"Fuck, I don't even want to be here anymore," I said out loud, the words slipping past my lips before I could control my tongue. Suddenly words filled my head, blasting my ears over and over, refusing to go quiet or even slow down.

Why do I even care anymore? My friends are all gone and now I have no one again. All I ever feel when I walk up these stairs is uncontrollable loneliness. I just want to be heard and to make people happy.

And more nagging questions: *Am I going to graduate? Did I succeed enough while being here in person?*

Words kept filling my mind, forming sentences, and stealing the air from my lungs as they came to the surface, where I battled them. When I got to the top of the stairs, I walked even more slowly to the office, the cracked concrete guiding my way.

Thoughts I hated the most started to fill my head: *Pathetic. No one likes you. Just leave, who's gonna notice? You will never amount to anything . . . ever.*

Like arrows stinging the walls surrounding my heart, the words always broke me down and set fire to everything. I would stand there burning with a fake smile plastered across my face.

If someone, just one person, would take a second to notice, they would see my smile drop the second I'm left with my own thoughts.

It felt like my brain was on fire whenever I was engaged in a conversation with anyone, like everything and everyone within a five-foot radius moved so much slower than I did. Sometimes I blew up like a stick of TNT, unable to control who I hurt and what I said.

I looked up and found myself at the school, as if my legs had brought me to my destination on their own. I quickly put on my fake smile and showed my teeth to my counselor as I passed, then sighed, picked up the clipboard, and signed myself in late.

I should have a stack of slips dedicated to me.

I swaggered my way into class, trying to keep my composure. I thought about all the people in the class, their eyes all beating down on me and judging me without ever saying a word.

That's what filled my mind: the daily thoughts and feelings of others. How did they perceive me? I kept looking around for the eyes I felt drilling holes in my soul. I knew the eyes weren't real, but the feelings and the fear in my mind were completely real to me.

Class time dragged by, and my thoughts poured gasoline over the flames in my head. Everything was full of smoke and soot.

Not only do the voices fill my head, but so do their faces, their voices, their attitudes—they all seem to live in my head. That's why I play music, why I can never get to sleep, why I sleep so much during the day, why I get high every morning, why it feels like I never care. Because no one wants to hear my voice. My grandma says I'm stupid. I'M SO TIRED OF NEVER BEING HEARD.

My ears perked up, hearing the dull ringing over and over that signaled the end of the period. I sighed, my thoughts finally leaving me because I had something new to focus on: filling my stomach. I picked up all my stuff from the grayish desk, looking around at all the paintings and colors on the wall. My eyelids felt heavy while I fought the urge to fall to the ground and sleep the rest of the day away.

If I could only forget about all the mistakes I've made.

I put my computer in my backpack, thumbed my finger on the volume button on my phone, and walked out of the warm classroom. I pushed past the kids crowding the old metal doors, kept my eyes on the concrete below, and told myself to stay awake.

I heard all their voices—the people around me and the people inside my head—over the sounds of loud music playing from my old headphones. Talking, talking, talking. Always talking.

I wanted to tell them all to shut up, to leave me alone. I wanted to disappear. I knew it wasn't them . . . but the voices always told me how much I was burning on the inside, how badly the fires spread and turned every thought and feeling into ash and smoke.

Keep calm. You got this.

As the thoughts filled my head, they flickered brightly, like a torch in a pitch-black room. "I got this . . . " I said under my breath, talking back to the voices. "Come on, you know you got this, we can make it another day."

I finally felt relief wash over me, like a dam opening and releasing the waves of calm and strength to wash the fires away. "Thank you . . ." I said slowly, finally being released from the voices, knowing that I would be safe from my mind while I ate lunch.

I walked through the old green cafeteria doors like I've done for years, grabbed my fruit cup, vegetable, and a slice of pepperoni pizza, then walked over to the side exit and looked around for people I knew. Finding no one, I made my way back over to the stairs heading down to the street.

I can't be there anymore.

When I reached the first step, I shot my hand in my pocket, looking for the little box of cigarettes. Five more steps, and I had one between my lips while I looked for my lighter. Ten steps, and the sound of the lighter flicked as a spark of fire jumped to life. Twenty steps, and the grayish smoke left my nose in a desperate escape to freedom.

All my feelings about the day—all the stress—faded for just a moment. But as I looked down at my hands and the smoke wafted up, the words began to fill my head again. They came slower this time; instead of a storm raging against the gates, it was a quiet stream.

I looked up toward the dark trees surrounding me and slipped my headphones on. I leaned back, letting my spirit drift into the never-ending search for new sounds, for something to soothe my soul again.

The same thing, every day. Exhaustion, like my bones were ready to shatter at the lightest touch, like my muscles screamed for rest while I still had a thousand miles to walk, like everything in my body hurt and just wanted to rest for good.

~ • ~

Some light arrived on a bright and sunny day the next summer, when I was first making money at my new job at Little Caesars down the road from my grandma's apartment. The weather had been hot for the past few days, and the clouds were almost nonexistent, so as I walked down the dry, cracked sidewalk I could feel the heat radiating from the ground. I thought it was gonna melt my shoes for sure. I had my work shirt on, with some black shorts, black Vans, a black-and-white Lakers cap, and my headphones. I hopped up to the edge of the curb, balancing on my toes and keeping my hands in my pockets while I hit my new disposable vape.

As I opened the door to work, I felt a cold wall slam into me from the air conditioning. I punched my card and number, then turned around to see a new person. They were thin, with slight muscles, and had dark red hair that was stuffed into a cap. They walked with their head low as if they didn't want to get in anyone's way; they avoided eye contact, and their face was covered by a black mask.

I slid my way back into the kitchen, my heart pounding so loud I could hear the blood rushing around my head. I smiled a little while I started making bread and saw the new person at the pizza prepare station. Different voices—not the negative ones—were screaming at me to go talk to them. Finally, I walked up to them and casually asked if they needed help. I had to take a deep breath to control my heart rate, then slid in and started helping them with pepperoni. My heart rate kicked up as I saw them reach up and tuck their hair behind their ear. My mouth felt hot and dry like the Nevada desert.

I finally choked out a greeting and my name, then asked, "What's your name?" The words came out of my mouth so quietly that I wasn't sure I had actually said them. They gave me a confused look.

I repeated the question a little louder as I fell deeper into their chocolate brown eyes. "Oh, I'm Azrael, but people call me Beef," they answered.

"Well, I'm gonna ask you a very serious question that may define the rest of our relationship."

They giggled a little and said, "Oh yeah, what's that?"

"What is your favorite color?"

"Red. Red is my favorite color."

"Nice to meet you Azrael. I hope we can get to know each other," I said with the biggest grin plastered on my face.

I couldn't get them out of my mind for days.

I felt happy, finally, and a week later I was nervous for a date for the first time in my life. I finally had a reason to leave the house, instead of wanting to sit in my room all summer just listening to sad songs about the way people suck and how life is just going to end soon. Suddenly I had something to look forward to.

~ • ~

I've been living with my birth mother in her new apartment for most of my senior year. She has been clean for over a year and a half. It's been great being with her; we talk about life and what to expect. It makes me so happy that she's clean and I can fix my relationship with her. We watch movies together, and she helps me with my car and getting to school. I appreciate her more every day. Even little interactions mean so much to me.

I am thankful that I can fix everything in my life. I hear the voices less and less often, to the point I don't even know if I remember what they used to say to me. I feel better being outside the house.

My life has gone up and down thousands of times in the past four years. It is crazy to think that I started at Scriber Lake High School four years ago, and now I'm leaving everyone behind to find my own future.

For now, my depression is gone. I'm ready for the real world.

A NOTE FROM TURTLE

My life started out in the best way possible, with two loving parents that loved each other, a big house, and amazing friends, but something changed in both my parents when they lost my little brother after a car accident. Both my parents started using drugs after this happened, and it destroyed our lives. I think about what could have been all the time. Today I'm doing better than ever. My youngest brother is living with my great-grandparents (though we'd rather he stayed with us). I have my best friend, Nathan Powell; I'd probably not be writing this story without him. I hope that someone finds my story helpful, that at least you know someone else has gone through shit just like you. Just let the music grasp the corners of your mind and pull you away, jump up with the beat, and dance with the flow of the world. Smile because you know you aren't alone in the world anymore, and you never have to be again. I want to use my love of music to go into a career in music engineering and make my way up to becoming a studio producer. I want to give something I love to everyone who feels shitty sometimes. I just hope the best for everyone in life. Thank you for listening to my story.

OPPOSITE
Jesus Ruiz, Untitled

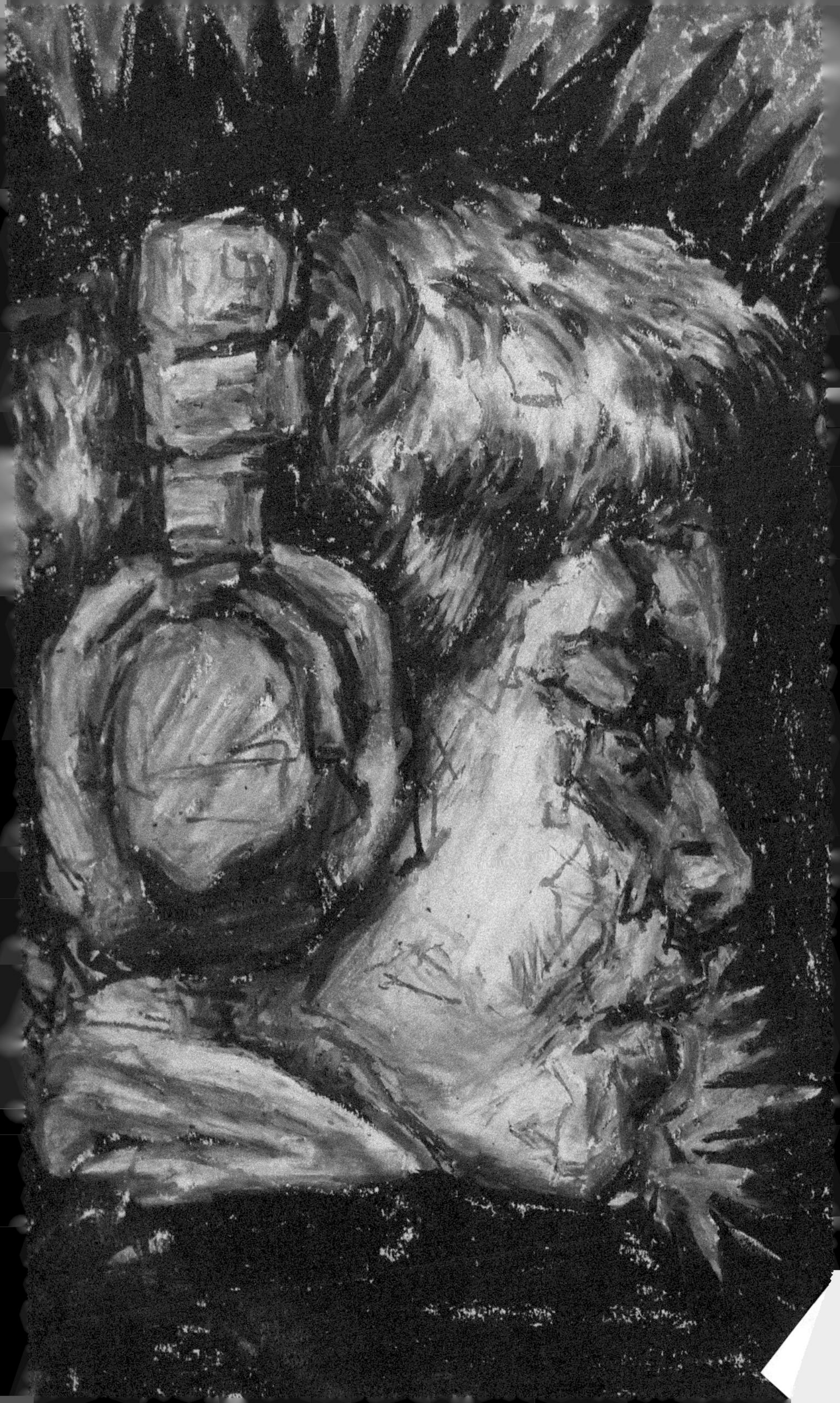

THEY'VE ALWAYS FOUGHT

Rhayne

5 Years Old

They've always fought.

I can't tell what they're arguing about this time. But as usual, I wake up in complete darkness, hiding under thick blankets, listening to hushed, angry arguing—as if they didn't somehow manage to still be loud enough to wake me up.

I'm so tired and I just want to go back to sleep. Their voices stress me out; there is no way I can ignore them. It's always some back and forth. It takes everything not to burst into tears. I'm five years old, and a bit of a crybaby. Any conflict sends my mind into a panic. I can't risk them hearing me, though. I hate that they drop whatever they're arguing about to coddle me.

I poke my head out of my blanket and see my fish tank lights shine throughout the whole room. My few goldfishes swim around the tank, their neon orange bodies contrasting against the fluorescent blue background. The bubbling of the filter doesn't drown out their voices, so I turn onto my side and throw a pillow over my head. The darkness and quiet is comforting in moments like these. It's nice to feel as if I am in an empty space, rather than in my own home.

~ • ~

9 Years Old

I am sitting on our old rocking chair in the living room of our Lake Stevens house. My two-year-old sister, Onyx, is already asleep in our room upstairs. My parents are arguing—sometimes screaming—with each other in the kitchen. I'm not listening to anything they say. I focus down on my white DS Lite, happily playing the Super Mario Bros. game my neighbors let me borrow.

Their voices get louder.

Suddenly I jolt to the sound of glass shattering on the cheap tile floors in the kitchen. I can't make out anything other than my dad screaming at my mom as she's yelling at him for throwing glass.

I don't want to be here anymore.

Closing my DS, I slide off the rocking chair and run up the stairs to my room. I shut the door behind me quietly so that I don't disturb my sister in her crib and climb onto the twin mattress next to it.

Our parents' voices grow louder once again as they come up the stairs. I cover Onyx's ears and stare at our door. They keep screaming at each other, and I hear a loud bang against our dryer.

My dad's yells fade as he walks down the stairs. Our mom must've convinced him to leave. It's quiet for a moment. I continue to stare blankly at our door as my mom rushes into our room. She says something as she lies down between Onyx and me, but I can't make it out. I watch her text someone.

**Can you call the cops?
Michael isn't being physical
but he's banging and hitting
shit.**

I don't know what to think. Before I know it, I hear my dad stomp up the stairs and fling the door open. The lights flick on. "I'm sick of your n**** bullshit!" he screams, slurring his words. I sit up immediately, shaking as I look between him and my mom with wide eyes. Her tears reflect on her pale skin.

"Go away, Mike! You're scaring the kids!" she yells back. Onyx is awake, but she doesn't react to the sounds around her. "You're hurting them!"

It doesn't matter. He continues to yell and rant as tears stream down his face, red with anger. I can't understand what is going on, but now Onyx is crying, and my mom is yelling more, and my dad is backing down.

My mom ushers us to get up and brings us into her room. I watch as she runs around and quickly gathers our clothes. She dresses us in another layer, then a big coat and shoes. She picks up Onyx and we make our way to the stairs. I take a good look around our house, at the glass shattered on our kitchen floor. My dad is nowhere in sight.

Commotion arises outside. I can hear my dad's voice speaking with strangers. My mom leads us outside. Two policemen are walking toward my dad, who is standing in our front lawn. Without stopping, my mom leads me and Onyx to my grandmother's red car. I try my best to take one last look behind me, but policemen are standing on both sides pointing flashlights on him. His curly hair hangs low, and he doesn't bother to face us as we leave. I get into my grandmother's car and look at my Uncle Dillon, who is sitting in the driver's seat.

We drive off the moment everyone is settled.

I don't see my dad for two weeks.

~ • ~

15 Years Old

"Rhayne!" my stepmom, Julia, calls.

I look up from my phone to see her standing by the front door of our home in Renton. She is heavyset with brown eyes and black hair, with freckles here and there on her brown skin.

"What?" I ask. I know exactly where this is heading.

"Wanna go to the store with me?"

I hesitate. *She wants alcohol. It's not even noon.* I remember all the promises made by both my dad and her. "No, this is our last weekend drinking! No more!" they swear up and down every weekend. Every time they get drunk, they fight endlessly until someone finally just goes to sleep. She looks at me expectantly.

Finally, I let out a sigh. "Yeah, sure. Let me grab a jacket."

Thoughts race through my mind as I walk through the small living room into my half-sister Elena's room. *The Land Before Time* plays on the TV on her chipped, white dresser. Elena is tending to herself, playing with her toddler dinosaur toys. I grab my yellow Cartoon Network hoodie and pull it over my head. It's freezing, yet I opt to wear my black shorts with my black Unus Annus tee.

I hear footsteps and keys jingling, so I walk out to meet Julia by the front door. She's wearing her maroon Graduating Class of 2012 hoodie, gray shorts, and black leggings.

My dad walks out of their bedroom, dab pen in hand, his face puffy and his now-rather-straight hair a mess; it looks like a troll doll's. He looks at us.

"Where the fuck are you guys going?" he grumbles, his voice low.

"To the store. I need to grab us a few things," Julia replies. I gave her a look.

He's not that stupid.

"You go to the store every weekend multiple times a day! What could we possibly be needing?"

"Milk. And I need more fruit for Elena."

My dad looks at me and shrugs. He sways slightly, still dealing with the consequences of drinking heavily the night before. Their financial issues, no matter how much my dad likes to vent about them to me, are not my problem. He lets out a sigh as he stumbles past us into the kitchen. Julia and I leave the front door wide open. I hesitate before walking out and turn back to Onyx, who is sitting at the kitchen table, watching TV.

"Do you want anything?" I ask.

"Root beer and candy," she answers, without looking away from the TV.

"Okay. Bye."

It's late summer, and it's still sunny out. We are both wearing hoodies and shorts when we hop into the black Yukon.

We go to Rite Aid first, where we head straight for the alcohol fridges near the back. She takes a couple bottles each for her and dad, then lets me pick something for myself. I give in; I want to drink. I find a large can of Mike's Hard Lemonade. I always get cranberry, otherwise the flavor mixed with alcohol grosses me out too much.

We start drinking in the car; I down the Mike's, and Julia throws back vodka shots. We go to a grocery store and buy what we need, plus more alcohol. We get even drunker.

At one point I stagger through an Albertson's to use the bathroom and had to be directed by staff members because I was so out of it. I don't remember leaving the Albertson's parking lot after downing another beer. At this point, I had probably had a couple Mike's, two shots, and a couple beers.

I don't remember getting home. I just remember being ushered to wake up because I had vomited while I was blacked out.

~ • ~

17 Years Old

I rush up the stairs of our Cle Elum townhouse. My dad, Julia, and Julia's daughter Elena just moved in, and it's a spacious place. It has an upstairs with two rooms—our parents' and Elena's. Onyx and I don't have a room because we only visit on the weekends. Our dog, Coco, sleeps next to us on the floor, where we've spread out blankets and pillows.

Tonight, my dad and Julia have been drinking a good amount of alcohol. When a fight breaks out, Onyx flees to Elena's room. But I stand and watch them argue, high out of my mind from the dab pen and the joints my dad bought for me earlier.

Elena always freaks out when she isn't with Julia. I know neither of them are capable of hurting her; they always manage to protect the children when one of them is more aggressive than the other. Somehow, they always steer clear of physically hurting us. As I open the white door, I see Onyx under the covers in the twin-size bed. Elena's toys are spread around the room.

"Are you doing okay, Onyx?" I ask as I walk toward the bed. I can hear muffled cries coming from under the blankets. My heart breaks in two.

She sits up, pulling the covers off her. Her freckled face is tear-stained, and when she sees me she starts crying again.

"No! They promised it would be a normal weekend! They promised they would stop drinking! They always break their promises!" she cries. She's choking through sobs.

Tears stream down my face, too. For the first time, I am at a loss for what to do. We've been in this cycle for five years and we need to get out so badly.

"I'm sorry, Onyx," I begin. My voice cracks.

"I know. I wanted it to be normal, too. So, so badly."

Noise erupts from downstairs. Onyx stares at the door before a look of horror washes over her face.

"Where's Elena?" she asks, looking around the room.

I paused for a moment before answering. "She's downstairs."

Onyx throws the covers off and begins to get off the bed. "We need to get her! We can't leave her down there with them. We need to get her up here!"

She jumps up and runs through the door and down the stairs. I follow her because I can't let her go to screaming adults all by herself. She's only ten, after all.

A convenience store bag and more alcohol bottles are cluttered on the counter. Julia and dad yell at each other with words incomprehensible to us. Julia, however, seems to be more sober than my dad. That's a plus.

The rest of the night is a blur, including complications around getting Elena to come upstairs. At some point, Julia decides to fall asleep on the living room floor and Elena goes back down to sleep with her. Onyx is upstairs, also fast asleep. It's just me and my dad.

"I called the cops on Julia," he says. I look at him, puzzled. He takes that as a cue to keep talking. "No, it's—we'll be okay. I told them we were smoking and they don't care about that. They just care about the violence."

His words slur as he speaks. I look him in the eyes. He isn't there. Whoever is looking back at me—it's not him.

He never actually called the cops, though. The police station is only a mile from our house, so they would have shown up right away. No one ever comes. My dad and I talk only briefly. I hold up a Cosmopolitan cocktail, premixed in a twelve-ounce glass bottle. The liquid is pink, and I adore the shape of the bottle with the corkscrew on top. My dad is on his phone, slowly pacing around the kitchen. Without a second thought, I pop off the corkscrew and take a couple big swigs from the bottle. The taste isn't as vodka-y as I expect it to be, and it doesn't burn as bad as whatever else they usually bring home. I chuckle before turning to my dad, holding the bottle high so he can see it from the opposite side of the counter.

"Can I take this home?" I ask, shaking the bottle.

My dad looks at me for a moment before nodding.

"Yeah. As long as she doesn't have it."

I don't take it. Something in me decides against it.

The following morning, nothing gets better. In fact, Onyx and I wake up to them yelling at each other again. Julia isn't drunk, or at least she's way more sober than she was before. My dad, on the other hand, is still gone. I roll my eyes as my dad begins to rant about my mother. How she makes him pay child support, how all the money is probably going toward her car, even her medical issues. Onyx, Julia, dad, and I are all standing around the kitchen island as he yells. My bag of things is lying flat on a chair and Onyx moves it to sit down. I don't know why, but I turn to her and begin scolding.

"Are you serious, Onyx? Do you not look before you sit?" I spit. I can see her facial expression change as she begins to defend herself when my dad jumps in.

"What the fuck is wrong with you?!" he yells, staring Onyx dead in the face. "All you had to do was just check where you were sitting. What the fuck, Onyx?"

Onyx begins to sob, choking out defenses, while Julia yells at my dad. I stare at the three in shock before turning to my dad, who is still screaming at Onyx.

"Shut up, it's not that serious!" I snap. He pauses for a moment and looks at me with his eyes wide. "She wasn't trying to cause a problem, she just didn't see it! She explained it herself. Why are you screaming at her?"

He starts yelling again. I let out an exhausted sigh and pull Onyx with me upstairs to Elena's room. We rush in, quickly closing and locking the door behind us. Footsteps echo through the house. I take my phone from my pocket and call my mom. It rings and rings, then—

I'm sorry, you've reached the voi—

I hang up. My heart beats through my chest as I look at Onyx. I shake my head, pressing the phone button on my mom's contact again. I try eight times with no response.

I begin to text her, hoping, praying to whatever Gods are watching that she'll answer. I send a few texts.

can u pick us up please??
they're super drunk and fighting
. . .
please they won't stop

No answer. The only other person I can think to call is my Uncle Devin. The phone rings and goes to voicemail.

can u help us contact mom??
please idk who else to ask

He's probably working, so my texts go unanswered.

We hear thumping up the stairs and hear a knock on the door. Both Onyx and I freeze, waiting for them to announce themselves.

"It's Julia." She jiggles the doorknob.

I don't really want to see her, but she's more tolerable than my dad in his current state. Onyx unlocks the door and Julia enters the room. The air is tense; I didn't know what to say.

"I'm sorry, you guys, I'm trying really hard to fight for you—" Julia begins, trying to give off a caring vibe. I cut her off.

"Please leave us alone. Both of you are fighting," I answer, my voice quavering.

She gives me a bewildered look as I begin walking toward the bathroom. Onyx follows behind me. I try to close the door behind us, but Julia pushes through.

"Really? I'm fighting for you guys out there and you don't

want to see me?" She is clearly offended.

I sigh, shaking my head. "Look, I'm just stressed out, I don't want to see either of you right now."

A look of disbelief washes over her face. "But I'm fighting—"

But she's cut off by the sounds of heavy footsteps coming up the stairs. My dad. The door swings open. All three of us look outside the bathroom door before walking out. My dad sways back and forth. He isn't seeing straight.

"I'm not the bad guy, Rhayne! I'm really not, tell them! Tell them I'm not the bad guy!" His pleas come out angrily. My heart drops as every word gets louder.

I burst into tears and bring my hands to cover my face because it is too embarrassing to cry in front of my dad. He yells again, but Julia steps in.

"What the fuck are you yelling at her for?" she snaps. "She's crying right now and you're yelling at her? Are you serious?"

Her words anger him more, and a string of hurtful things I can't comprehend come out of his mouth.

Two hours later, my mom finally arrives. She comes into the house yelling.

"You promised you wouldn't put your hands on her like you did to me!"

They argue for the next twenty minutes, then my mom, Onyx, and I finally make it out to her car and get in. Both my dad and Julia follow behind us, leaving Elena behind. I turn my head to look at my dad as he walks up to the car. My mom rolls down her window to continue saying things to him, but my dad looks at me and pleads, "Rhayne, please, I'm not the bad guy. Tell them I'm not the bad guy." I hold back more tears.

"Goodbye, Michael," my mom says while backing up. Julia begins dragging my dad away from behind, trying to get him inside. My heart pounds in my chest, my ribs rattling with every beat.

I can hear him yell as we drive away, but I don't look back. The tension is heavy as we drive in silence. I break it to let out a sigh of relief.

I don't have to deal with my dad like that anymore.

~ • ~

Still 17 Years Old

We sit around the campfire at Riley Lake playing Rage Cage, a drinking game. My grandma planned this trip for me, Onyx, my cousins, my uncle and his friends, and my mom and her boyfriend. It is dark outside, the only light coming from the neighboring campsites.

My cousin Lily and I are super drunk. Lily's so tired she heads to bed early. My younger cousin, Gavin, and Onyx had gone to sleep way earlier leaving me, my mom, her boyfriend, my grandma, my uncle, and his friends around the fire. They are praising me for being such a good sister to Onyx.

"She thinks I hate her!" I choke out, my words slurring as I speak. "I don't, I really don't. I've only wanted to protect her!"

My mom shoots me an empathetic look. "She doesn't think you hate her," she says, trying to comfort me.

I don't understand why I'm so emotional, but I continue to sob. I feel guilty. It hits me; I've hurt my little sister by protecting my dad. I've defended him over and over and have never spoken about anything that happened all those years at his place. I can't stop thinking about it. I risked her for my father's sake—for a man who has probably just been constantly lying to me.

"Mom," I begin, trying to wipe away my tears, ignoring everyone else at the campsite besides her. "I'm sorry. I never really hated you all those years, dad just—" I continue to weep, everything coming out in pieces, tears streaming down my face. "I don't know . . . he's lied all this time. I'm sorry, I really am."

She looks at me, surprise written all over her face. I'm sure she wasn't expecting to hear this; I certainly wasn't expecting to say it.

"It's okay, Rhayne. I figured it was something with your dad. But I never blamed you. I love you, okay?"

I nod, leaning back in my camping chair. "I love you, too."

I'm exhausted. I finally zone in on everyone else and can feel their eyes on me. I just want to go to bed. I sigh and stand up, dusting off my large black coat. "I'm going to bed. Goodnight, guys."

I exchange hugs with people, then stumble off, sighing with relief. This is it. No more lying about my dad, covering up for him, defending him. People have to know. I'm not daddy's little girl anymore.

I kick off my shoes, unzip the tent, and climb inside. Lily, Gavin, and Onyx are already passed out. I climb into my spot beside Lily and struggle with the sleeping bag before slipping into it. I pull a portion of the big blanket we share on top of me before eventually rolling over to my side.

It's a nice feeling to go to bed drunk tonight.

I enjoy how heavy I feel as I sink into the mattress.

What a night. A night that I don't have to deal with in the morning.

~ • ~

18 Years Old

I look at my dad as he pulls into our driveway. This is our first time seeing each other in person since his arrest in November. He's been out of jail since February, but no plans were made until April.

He picks us up from our mom's house and drives us to a park to walk around. He and Onyx play basketball while I watch, being sure to record short little moments with my phone. We go to my work to eat food with my discount, paying with the money our grandparents from his side gave us.

I feel strange. The energy feels different. It's no longer comfortable.

Maybe this feeling will improve over time.

My dad doesn't seem too interested in changing. He still makes the same jokes, still asks the same invasive questions. I have learned that I don't have to forgive him, though. I don't have to sit there and tell him it's okay if he fucks something up.

That's not my job. I've been through enough trying to console my ex-boyfriend when he made mistakes. No need to do it for my dad.

I'm still in a place of hurt. Even in that hurt, he's still my dad. I still have some feelings of love for him, despite everything he's put me through.

I lean back into the leather chair of his tan Escalade, and I hit my vape before shoving it into my pocket, turning my head to blow it out the cracked window. My dad doesn't say anything. I don't know if he doesn't care, or if he doesn't feel like he can say anything now that I am 18.

"Thank you for letting me pick you guys up," he says when we pull up to our house. He smiles when he looks at me, then my sister. We both nod.

"Thank you for all this, dad. It was nice seeing you again," I reply, anxiously shifting in my seat. I am ready to get inside. My sister says her thanks and my dad gestures for us to hug him. I unbuckle my seatbelt to give him a side hug before backing up so Onyx can get close enough to hug him, too. Every emotion I feel makes my stomach flip.

Brian, my counselor at school, told me I don't have to include him in my life, that it isn't my obligation. And he's right. However, at this moment, I realize he is just a man trying to keep a connection with his kids. Even after everything, he still somewhat tries to make us happy. I don't have to forgive him; I don't have to do anything. But I can at least appreciate the moment with my dad.

"I love you guys," he says, smiling as he looks at Onyx, then at me.

I hesitate for a moment, and I wonder if he notices.

"I love you too," I say.

"I love you too, dad," Onyx replies, leaning forward from the back to give him one last hug. I smile at my dad before grabbing the door handle and hopping out. Onyx and I walk up the driveway.

I don't know if I'll ever completely heal the wounds he's caused, but I will never let what happened turn me into what he became.

A NOTE FROM RHAYNE

My dad came to my graduation in June 2023. I only saw him for a few minutes, but he met Brian, and he told me I did a good job. He drove three hours from his home to see me and I appreciate the time he put in. We don't talk much. He occasionally sends me a "miss you and love you" text, and I'm always sure to respond.

I wasn't sure I would ever finish this story. I started working full-time immediately after graduation and went back into a hellish cycle of sleep between shifts. I have been trying to improve myself; I'm making plans to move out to live with a friend! I'm hoping to finally get my license in 2023 and stop working at Dairy Queen. I would also like to give a shout-out to my animals who passed away. Smokey died in August 2022, right before everything went down. I wanted to find a way to include her in this story but couldn't, so I thought I'd mention her here. I love you and miss you, Smokey baby. And to Roxy, my childhood dog who was with us for almost all of my young life, passed away on April Fools' in 2021. I hope you are resting well; I wish you could've been with me to see me graduate. I love you.

"I remember thinking my father was
mean but knowing he was kind. I
remember thinking my father was kind
but knowing he was mean."
—Mary Ruefle, "Woodtangle"

carry it all.

REVERSE
Jesus Ruiz, Untitled

CRADLING GRIEF

Wisteria Ray

"Roll initiative!" Anthony's voice booms.

I smile at my uncle, and he smiles back. He sits at the head of the dining table behind the D&D dungeon master's screen, where he commands the room with his large frame, loud voice, and a laugh that shakes the house. The table is full of family and friends: my brother, my dad, my cousins, and my three uncles—the cousins and uncles not blood-related. You can tell just by looking at them: Anthony's black skin, Birdy and Chad's white skin, and my dad's somewhere-in-between skin. But blood never mattered to us. My uncles learned early that a good friend is worth more than a thousand biological family members who didn't understand you. They learned that if someone supported you, knew when to push you, and felt like home, they were family.

"Okay, who rolled between 25 and 20? 20 and 15?" Anthony demands. "No one? Slackers."

He puts us in order for the battle. We imagine our characters and the space around them, placing ourselves on the battlefield. As I stare down at my list of spells, the tension in the room is thick enough to cut with a knife. Preparing for my turn, I choose the spell my wizard will cast—my favorite. Anthony looks at his notebook and declares it to be my turn next. I point at him dramatically and say, "I cast . . . Crown of Madness!"

My dad places a hand on my shoulder in support. Anthony feigns fear as he rolls the die that will decide the bandit's fate. The die clatters against the wood table and settles behind the screen where the players can't see it. Anthony, from his side of the screen, declares it a 10. The rest of my found family cheers because that number means the bandit is now mine to control.

The way Anthony looks at me makes me feel like I am his favorite person in the world.

I wonder if he ever lies about the rolls of the dice. I wonder if he lies in my favor.

~ • ~

"Did you know Anthony has cancer?"

"No," my mom answered, "I didn't." She put down her book and kept a blank face while her eyes scanned my body language.

I stared at her. I didn't really understand what I was saying, I just knew that it was true. I had put all the pieces together once Anthony mentioned chemo earlier that day. I was filled more with anger than with fear. I was angry that no one had told me. I had cut off that side of the family a long time ago due to a messy falling-out, and then rejoined just a year ago. They welcomed me back with open arms, despite how nervous I was to see them again. My brother told me that I had betrayed my family by leaving, and I believed him . . . until I stepped into that house again—the house I had grown up visiting. When I walked through the door, Anthony was the first to welcome me.

"Glad to have you back!" he shouted with his signature enthusiasm.

I hadn't spoken to Anthony in years during the time apart, except for a few words at a party. Before the separation, I was a little kid. But when I learned that he was sick and dying, my stomach felt like it was filled with lava, and there was heat behind my eyes. I only found out because I heard one of my uncles joke with him about having six months to live, and then later, when he mentioned the chemo, I knew for sure.

No one really told me anything about Anthony's condition because I was the baby of that group, and they never wanted to tell me bad news. All I knew was that he wasn't projected to die for a year, and I had hope that the chemo would work.

~ • ~

When I walked in the door at my Uncle Birdy's house, Anthony was sitting in his soft brown recliner as usual. But he groaned in pain as he stood and opened his arms for a hug.

"Gimme some sugar!" his voice boomed.

His head was shaved and littered with bald patches. When I hugged him, I noticed he had lost weight. This was the first time he looked sick to me. I knew chemotherapy did those things, but if he was on chemo, he was sure to get better—right?

My uncle continued disintegrating before our eyes. After losing his hair and the weight, he started to lose his mind. We had to stop playing D&D; he was our dungeon master, and he was either too tired to play or couldn't get his mind right to plan our sessions.

My fear grew as the rest of the year creeped by. I had never lost someone this close to me. I had lost grandparents that I barely knew, but I never processed their deaths. My dad had, though. Watching him grieve his parents made me realize how hard death hits a loved one. At least, I knew how hard it hit my dad. I knew that he drank until he either forgot or felt a little better. Losing a brother would hurt him so much more; I hoped losing Anthony wouldn't kill him.

I hoped it wouldn't kill me.

I was feeling a thousand emotions swirling inside my stomach. I always did the same thing when I felt that way. I turned to writing.

You are the first tragedy I did not want to write about.
You are the first family member to die that
I am not conflicted about.
You are not dead yet,
This poem will be different when you are.

Because you are alive,
I will try not to mourn you.
Because you are alive,
I will not grieve just yet.

I will stop crying and instead ask you
What your favorite color is.
I want to know.
I'm going to want to know.

I am going to tell you
what an amazing uncle you are,
I want you to know.
I'm going to want you to know.

I will ask for your best stories so I can
Tell them as best as I can.
All the things you want to scream,
I will scream for you.

And I will mourn you.
I will grieve.

When it is time.

~ • ~

Before I knew it, a barbeque was planned at my dad's house—except everyone knew it wasn't actually just a barbeque. It was a goodbye event. Anthony was dying. He knew the end was soon. I was bouncing off the walls in anger because I was scheduled to work. I was a rule-follower, and I didn't even think about calling out. When I told my manager about my troubles, he told me it would be fine if I left early. I almost cried with joy. I was desperate to see Anthony again.

Once my shortened shift was up, I raced down the freeway to my uncles' house. When I walked in, Anthony was sitting in his reclining chair. I waited for him to get up to greet me, but quickly realized he didn't have the strength. He just opened his arms and whispered, "Gimme some sugar."

He couldn't shout anymore. I hugged him while holding back tears. He was completely bald, had lost an insane amount of weight, and his skin was frighteningly pale. The loss of his voice shook me most; he had always been the voice of reason.

But he was still alive, and I held onto that fact with a grip that made my knuckles go white.

Soon after I arrived, Anthony got so tired he had to go to bed. He missed most of the barbeque. I spent the time trying to socialize with the adults and trying not to cry. Grief was already infecting me. It was in my digestive system. My stomach tied itself in knots.

Before leaving, I made my way upstairs to see him. His son was standing beside the bed. Anthony looked so weak. So tiny. He used to be big and strong and now he was not.

"Hey," he whispered.

The lump in my throat grew. I thought I might throw up.

"Sadly, I'm going to have to step down as dungeon master. My voice isn't what it used to be. Don't worry, someone else will take over. Do you have any ideas for how I could still play without talking as much?" he asked.

"Well, one time I played a game and someone played as another character's familiar. He was just a wolf that fought in our battles. You could do that," I responded, hopefully.

His face lit up.

"That sounds like a great idea. I'll see you in the next session."

His joy infected me and all my worries disappeared.

"See you. I love you!"

"Love you too."

I left in high spirits, knowing I would see my uncle again, knowing that things would go back to normal.

~ • ~

A month later, I was sitting on the couch watching *Survivor* with my mother, my stepfather, and my stepsister. I felt an energy in the air, a darkness in the room. I assumed my parents had been fighting—not because they ever did, but because that was the only logical explanation for the darkness.

I had a soft blanket wrapped around me as we laughed, pointed, and made accusations and observations. When the contestant was voted off and we were told to "tune in next time,"

I turned to the others to suggest playing a board game. But I didn't get a word out before my stepdad suggested my sister take a walk with him.

I remember thinking that she was in deep water, so I shot her a sympathetic smile as they got on their shoes, coats, and walked out the door. Once they were gone, I turned to my mom for an explanation.

Then I saw her face. Her eyes were filled with tears and regret. I knew Anthony was dead.

She got up from the couch and moved toward me like I was a wild animal that might run away at any moment. I was already crying when she arrived. Her voice was gentle, but loud enough to hear over my sobs. She told me he had died 40 minutes earlier.

I wailed.

~ • ~

The next day I was deep in denial.

I went to school and hung out with my friends. I even made a joke about my uncle's passing. My family stared at me like I was going to break any second. But I didn't. That came the following day.

When I woke up, I just stared at the ceiling until I started crying. My mom didn't try to talk me out of it; she just let me stay home. I spent the day crying or distracting myself from crying. That's how I spent the day after that, too. And the weekend. When Monday rolled around, my mom told me I had to go to school.

"I can't," I said, tears dripping down my face.

"You have to."

I couldn't believe her. How did she not understand? I knew she had experienced death before, but now she doesn't get it? I am grieving now. I am a grieving person, and I felt like I was nothing more than that. I was no longer a creative person, a fashionable person, a kind person, a loved and loving person. Suddenly I was just a grieving person. And the world was moving on without me. I had missed two days of school, and now I had to go back?

I was angry at my mother for pushing, I was angry at myself for grieving, and I was angry at Anthony for dying. He wasn't supposed to die. He was the sober one. The one guy who was sober for years in my family. His brothers' bodies were riddled with alcohol and drugs, and he was the one to get cancer and die.

He was the only one who could get me through this grief. He had a way of helping everyone with hard emotions. He was an addiction counselor, after all. But he was dead. And I was angry.

~ • ~

You have died.
I have begun grieving.
The others found ways to press pause.

They drink, and ingest, and pop.
They find people who will make them smile.
Make them forget.
But not me.

Instead, I have been cremated alongside you.
I sit on my mother's mantle and
Hear her talk to my ghost, saying
"You have to come back to me."
"You have to remember how to live."

I pull the blankets farther up my withered corpse.
My hair has begun to fall out.
I have not decided if I prefer feeling empty or angry,
But something has to replace my heart.

You have died.
I have grieved,
And I will grieve.

How dare you.

~ • ~

Dropping out of school seemed like the only option. I fought with my mom every morning and hated school. It lasted too long and required me to be more than a grieving person. I still attended drama class with a smile, but I could do nothing more. I eventually found a way to technically stay in school: doing independent work at home. It was kind of like online school, but with little to no contact with people. I hated that, too, but it was my only choice if I wanted to graduate on time. And I knew Anthony would hate to see his death stop me from my future. So I trudged on.

The school year did not end with a bang. It fizzled. I stayed in my house nearly every day and didn't finish my independent work. I just gave up, and everyone let me. At some point that spring, before I shut myself in, I skipped school for the very first time and headed to the library. There, I read grief and loss books until my brain felt full. I learned many things that gave me comfort, even if many of them weren't super helpful. Most of them were secretly religious and claimed that my uncle had moved on to heaven. I liked believing that was true, but it never lasted long. Heaven wasn't real to me, even if I believed my uncle was still watching out for me. The books declared that with some prayer and some visits to church, everything would get better. That didn't ring true either, so I focused on some of the other lessons. The one that stuck with me most is that grief is just another form of love, similar to a hug or affectionate words.

I grieve because I love him, and loving him is grief.

~ • ~

Recovery was slow. Over the summer, I visited family and worked at the Alderwood Mall. I walked by the huge sign for a restaurant, the big red letters reading "Anthony's," at least twice a week, and it always made me feel a sorrow deep in my stomach. But, eventually, it was just a restaurant. Not a sign, or a reminder, but a place with seafood and most likely underpaid workers. One day when I was playing D&D with my family, my dad offhandedly told a story about Anthony and the trouble they got into, and I laughed instead of cried. When the Super Bowl came around, I didn't pay attention. I never did. But it made for a good day at work, since the mall was nearly empty. When I came home seven hours later, my mom ran up to me.

"Guess who won?"

"Mom, I don't care."

"The Chiefs!"

It didn't hit me until she continued.

"The Kansas City Chiefs! Anthony's team!"

I smiled. I wasn't sad he missed it; I was happy for the reminder that my uncle loved that team. I had totally forgotten. But in my memories of him, in nearly every one, he wore a hat with the Chiefs' logo on it. My mom and I cheered.

The necklace I often wore, a silver chain with forget-me-nots encased in resin, became a symbol of carrying him with me instead of me just missing him. I even stopped wearing it when it clashed with my outfits. I didn't need a physical attachment to him anymore.

~ • ~

It was the way Anthony smiled. It was the way he would make fun of my uncle Birdy for cooking dinner so late. It was in the way he told stories. It was that he loved the Kansas City Chiefs, and the way he didn't love drinking water. It was how he screamed "Well, fuck her!" when my girlfriend broke up with me. It was in the way he loved me that made it so easy to love him back. There were just so many reasons to love him.

Once, he agreed with me in a moment that probably didn't matter much to him. My older brother and I were fighting and it triggered my PTSD, so I had begun crying. When Anthony saw me, he pulled me aside and said, "Y'know, I don't like him very much, either."

I realized that my wonderment and attachment to that moment stemmed from the fact that it was mine. It used to be a shared moment, private to the two of us, but then it became only mine. Did his brothers know he said that? Probably not. He made me, with a single sentence, feel so much better. He had a way of doing that. He always knew what to say. I admired that about him because I never had that trait. I hold onto words until I forget them or they are no longer necessary or appropriate.

If I had been braver, I would have talked to Anthony more near the end. If I was braver, maybe I wouldn't have left the family all those years ago. Perhaps I would have had years with him, instead of small words at a party and not enough game nights. I never did ask him for his favorite color, or for his best stories. But I didn't find the lack of knowing those things overly sorrowful or hurtful; I just saw it as a fact of life. I knew that I was healing, and I welcomed it. I welcomed the moments that reminded me of him, and the love I felt for him was as strong as ever.

~ • ~

Eleven months later, I woke up from a nightmare. In it, I was sitting at my uncle Birdy's dining table with my family. It was like it had been before Anthony died. Everyone around me was laughing and talking to each other, rolling dice and casting spells. The only thing different was Anthony. He sat at the head of the table, like always, and led the game. But his face was blurry, like it had been erased in Photoshop. I could tell he was opening his mouth and speaking because everyone at the table would respond, but I couldn't hear his voice. When I woke, I realized that my greatest fear was coming true. I was forgetting him.

I wept nearly as hard as I did on the day he died.

I knew the day would come. It had been a year since I'd seen him at the barbeque. It had been nearly a year since he died. I frantically looked at pictures of him until my memory was jogged and his face returned to me. But his voice? The voice of reason, the voice that commanded a room, the laugh that shook the house? It was gone. I was 17 when he died, and I was 18 when I began to forget. What about when I'm 20? 30? 40? Will he be completely lost to me? Grief is all I have left of him; will I lose even that?

I threw myself into grief as an apology for my mistakes. I began crying every day again just to remember his face. I didn't know if this was healthy and I did not care. I did not want to get better anymore if better meant I had to be without him.

His name was Anthony, and I loved him enough to grieve.

~ • ~

I want to believe you are in Heaven.
I want to believe you are an Angel.
I want to believe you are still you and
You are still here,
Not as a ghost,
But as holy light.

But the anger I felt after you died was more biblical than
You will ever be.
It was radiant and damaging.
It was Wrath and Greed and Pride.

I truly believe you could not live peacefully in Heaven if
You saw me.
You'd break down the gates and
Run down the steps
But you haven't embraced me yet,
So I know you are not there.

I hold you like I used to hold God.
Not willing to let go of what was,
What could have been.
Wishing for him to hold me back,
Wishing for him to hear my voice,
I pray to you.

I pray to you,
Please come back.
Please be a spirit that watches over me.
Please let my anger leave me.

You believed in heaven, so why can't I?

~ • ~

Hello again, dear Journal.

It's the one-year anniversary. But you knew that already. I avoided everything all day until I got home from work. That's when I cried. I cried because he never saw me cry over him. I cried for the siblings who didn't really know him. I cried for my brother who loved him but couldn't come to the memorial. I cry because we're a "no crying" family and I'm scared Anthony never cried in front of anyone. I'm scared he was ashamed and afraid and never told anybody. Was he terrified? I can't believe we made jokes and we commented and we said goodbye but never cried together. I hope he cried with his brothers the way I am crying now. I hope he found peace before it happened. I hope he didn't die afraid.

Mom says I'm carrying him with me. But I don't want him to be with me; I want him to be with his body, in his house, with his brothers and a set of dice. I want to make him laugh again. I want to see the laugh lines on his face. I want to cry with him over his death. I want him to hold me and teach me about his death and how to handle it. He was the only one who could've said the right thing. I'm sure of it.

I miss him in the way I miss myself.

I hold grief the way I want to hold him.

I cradle grief until we both say, "I'm sorry."

carry it all.

A NOTE FROM WISTERIA

Anthony was an amazing man. But I had to let him go. And, for the most part, I have. Writing this story has been incredibly healing for many reasons. It helped me understand him more, it helped me understand myself, and it keeps his story alive. I will always miss him, but it is no longer devastating. I still think about him, write about him, and talk about him to anyone who cares to listen. Grief does get easier. Like the addictions Anthony counseled, there are ups and downs. There are days when you fall back into that pit of despair. But I learned tools to help me crawl back out of it.

I'm very excited to be graduating this year. Even though I had many times when I thought I would drop out, I persevered. I hope my story is helpful in any way, whether you relate to or you now understand what someone else is going through. If I had to give one piece of advice to someone helping someone else through grief, it would be to let the person cry. Let them feel all the emotions and listen if they want to talk. And if you are going through grief, I recommend writing about it. Trust me, it helps.

carry it all.

REVERSE
Jesus Ruiz, Untitled

PIECES

K

I wasn't sure if publishing this story was possible for me. It's so intimate and deeply personal to an inner world I'm familiar with, yet it feels difficult to explore while thinking about sharing it publicly. For this reason, I was not able to finish my story. My intention for including pieces of it here is to help people feel less alone. As isolating as your experience feels, there is someone out there who can connect with it and you.

Before you read, I want you to know there are some vivid scenes that include suicidal ideation that may potentially be triggering if you aren't in a safe place within yourself to hear it. If you feel you have space for my story, I hope as you hold it, your own story may feel a little less heavy. I know mine does. If you're not in the right space, that's okay. Come back when you're ready.

Letter to My Younger Self

Dear Buttercup,

How's your mind?

That question may confuse you. I don't know if anyone's ever told you, but you think too much. If someone has, did they tell you it's one of your biggest gifts? Eventually, you'll be able to let those wild thoughts of yours be, and in turn, you will learn how to just be, too.

How's your heart?

You know it's large, you know it hurts. I know you long to love, and heal, and help. I hope you know you're meant to know the love you already have within you.

When's the last time you felt understood?

I know sometimes it's hard to feel like you fit into this world. I know life seems tedious, and you feel lost and confused and alone. That's a scary feeling. But you're expansive, bright, and limitless. I know that's scary sometimes, too. I hope you know you're safe. No matter where you are in this world—whether it's where you're standing, or in the world your mind has created—no amount of fear or hurt will ever touch you deep enough to kill you.

Because above all else, you will learn that you are held in this confusing place. You're tethered deeply to this life and everything around you in ways you will never fully understand, and you'll learn to be okay with it.

You'll keep your questions, and you'll find comfort in a few answers. You'll trust yourself, your heart, and your mind. I take care of you, and you take care of me. I'm learning more about you for the both of us. So be where you are; I'll help you pick up the pieces. Presence is your friend. I promise. And if the answer to the last question is that you don't feel understood, I hope you know I get you. I got you.

I've always been with you.

You are my light, friend.

Piece One: Yellow Light, Age 10

Why do we die? When do we die? I don't want to die. I'm going to die.

I don't understand why I'm here. I don't understand why I have to leave.

Another sleepless night, kept up by swirly thoughts. The weight of existence was heavy, too much for my ten-year-old body. Images flooded my senses: Waking up in a casket, the people at my funeral. Drowning in the bathtub, the knives in the kitchen. Death by my own hands. Darkness. Nothingness—the most terrifying feeling.

Suicide.

No. No. No.

I don't want to die. I'm going to. I can't do this anymore, what if I just . . . ?

My feet followed my thoughts and my eyes to the kitchen light ahead. I slipped out of my pink sheets and zebra-patterned fluffy comforter quickly and stiffly. Like a moth drawn to a flame, I felt the rough brown carpet beneath my bare feet and heard the creaking of the old floors until I was on the cold, gray-tiled hallway. I made my way through the dining room all the way to the kitchen, where I stood with my feet pointed straight at the knives. I was frozen in fear—flooded by the thoughts, feelings, and sensations on my wrist of what I believed I was about to do. I stood stone cold on the tile floor in the yellow lit kitchen for minutes, listening to my soft, choppy breath.

My heart pounded.

Who will find me?

Just do it.

What comes next?

I'm scared. I'm scared of nothingness. Although living feels dark too.

I'm scared of it all. Why am I here? Why can't anyone tell me why? Doesn't anyone else feel this? I don't want to be scared anymore.

Help.

Finally, something allowed me to break free. My sight went blurry and before I knew it, I was lying stiffly in my bed again, staring at the same yellow light peeking through my doorway, reaching from the kitchen toward my bed. It was sharp and pointed, barely touching the edge of the bed on the floor, almost saying "stay" in the same way that it had said "come" earlier.

I don't remember falling asleep, and I don't remember what came next. Maybe it was darkness, but I know somewhere down the line there was light.

Piece Two: I'm Still Here, Age 11

I didn't tell anyone about that night. I was hoping the memory of it would just go away. But the confusion lingered into the next year.

I was sitting in my assigned seat in the very back of my fifth-grade classroom, taking in my classmates' fresh new outfits as the jitter of a new beginning flowed through the room. I observed the new students, including a blonde girl with freckled, tan skin sitting to my right. I noticed how pretty my teacher was and admired her long, brown, wavy hair. I noticed which students seemed happy to be there, and the ones whose heads were a little lower, who seemed already ready to go home.

I scanned each side of the room and admired the neat way the classroom was set, and wondered if it had always been this way, or if the teacher had changed it for her new class. I turned around halfway while she was speaking and saw all the books I had yet to discover. I felt the warm sunshine gleaming through the large windows onto the side of my right cheek. There was a bright sensation in my body.

A lift, a realization. And then . . .

Oh shit.

The light was then met with a melancholy feeling and a darker, untouched memory from the summer.

I'm still here.

I'm here.

If I would've gone through with it that night, I wouldn't get to experience this newness, these people, this sunshine. Life would have gone on without me.

I wondered if anyone saw me drifting as the darkness consumed the light.

I tried not to let myself get too sucked into the wonders of "what if."

I'm just glad I'm here.

Piece Three: Foreign Familiar, Age 14

"Are you depressed?"

The words felt like a flick in the head, a sting to my already sensitive being.

I didn't like the word.

I stared back at my eighth-grade PE teacher with my defenses rising, separating the air between us.

"No."

"You sure?" Mr. T's tone was awkward and unsure. His grin did not match the weight of the question he was asking.

"Yes." My vision narrowed at the dirty ground, trying to hold back tears I didn't understand. My thoughts scattered through the echoing voices and squeaky shoes bouncing off the walls and the gym floors.

"Do you want to talk to someone? A friend? A counselor?"

"No. I just want to sit here."

"Okay, I'm going to get a counselor."

I had been Mr. T's student for a year already. Since the beginning of seventh grade, he had challenged me because he knew I was up for it. I was a student athlete in sports all year round.

This year, though, I was falling asleep during warmups, and I wasn't dressing down for class. I chalked it up to the difference in class period, from sixth to first, but truly, I just didn't want to admit that there was a lot of hurt in me.

The counselor I met with that day told me what I was feeling was because of my cycle. She dismissed me and I left feeling smaller than before.

I was failing all my classes, both honors and regular. I was sleeping all the time, mostly hours I shouldn't have been, like during school and after. That left the night to myself. Sports were my outlet; my journal was too. That's when I began to try to write out these foreign, familiar feelings.

Those feelings didn't make it out much further from those pages, and the most confusing stuff stayed within me.

Piece Four: "Help," Ages 15 and 16

Darkness lingered. It wouldn't be ignored. It wanted help.

I needed help.

I checked out of high school two months into my freshman year—a few months before the Covid lockdown.

I fell off the face of the earth and let go of the friendships and hobbies I had built in middle school. Nobody really gave my lack of presence much thought, or at least not that I knew of. *People have lives of their own.* I was back to believing mine wasn't worth continuing.

So without truly saying goodbye to life, I said goodbye to my participation with the life I had been living, and began one that stayed in the confinements of my mind and the four walls of my bedroom.

After I stopped going to school, I found an outlet in marijuana. It was a feeling that brought me out of the turmoil of existence and into a euphoric place. I was hooked. It helped me. It was my medicine.

A few months later, I lay on top of a fuzzy gray and white blanket with LED purple lights filtering everything in my bedroom.

I knew the thoughts, the feelings.

I was frozen again, in the same bed that had held me five years before. But this time I picked up the phone and made a call.

"I don't know if I can be here any longer," I told my friend.

It took her less than five minutes to be at my place. She met me on the couch. I unraveled in her arms. She was sure I was going to kill myself.

Before I knew it, I was out of my room, through the yellow living room, and into a hospital bed.

Out of the purple, through the yellow, and into white.

Quiet.

~ • ~

"You remind me of me when I was your age," the social worker said. Tears formed in their eyes as I stared back. I felt held. Seen.

"I don't feel safe. I don't trust myself," I answered.

That's all they needed to know.

Before admitting me to Fairfax Behavioral Health, they said, "I hope I never see you again."

They smiled with sympathy and light in their eyes.

I understood.

I hope you never see me here again, either, I indicated with a nod.

I didn't see that social worker again. Not because that was my last time in that space, they just weren't there the second time around.

I was much less there, as well.

When marijuana and I became friends, we became inseparable. I spent most of my days with them, breathing in and tasting mother nature's flower. Smoke filled my days, and fog found my mind. I needed it. I needed to not see.

That's not fair though, is it? To deny my existence at its rawest form is almost worse than feeling it all.

The suppression of my thoughts and feelings was beginning to really take a toll on my body. Everything felt muted.

~ • ~

Six months later I sat in my friend's room on a red couch, hitting their dab pen. The room started to become fuzzy, and I felt like I was closing in on myself. There was a bubbling sensation blocking my throat, and a jolt of energy originating from the core of my chest and diaphragm up into my neck. A sharp "huh" sound escaped from my mouth as my neck flipped forward. It was like something knocked the wind out of me—not incredibly uncomfortable, just something that needed to get out.

My friend looked at me with confusion mixed with amusement because the sound I made was funny. But I continued to fold over myself ever so slightly in whole-body hiccups.

I didn't know what was happening.

When the tics continued, I texted my dad and asked him to pick us up and take us both back to my house.

"What the fuck?" My dad turned from the driver's seat and looked at me, confusion twisting his features, as I jolted forward every minute or so from my core, odd sounds coming from my mouth. I couldn't get a full sentence out to explain it, though. Even if I could have talked, I wouldn't have been able to explain it.

My body had taken my voice.

A NOTE FROM K

After about 24 hours of experiencing and developing new verbal and motor tics, I was admitted to the psych ward for the second time. My mental state had continuously worsened, and it wasn't until my body started to speak that I had no choice but to listen. My second stay lasted ten days. At the time, I was really fighting my existence, but something in me knew I wasn't finished being here. I just needed to learn to really *be here.* Although that stay was brief, it actually was the catalyst for deeper parts of my healing journey.

I know this story touches on a lot of darkness, but I promise you, the darkness and the light were not as far apart as I felt they were. It's been almost three years since my first and last time in the ward, and my life has changed drastically. Mostly my relationship to myself, and in turn to the world around me.

As I mentioned, this story is unfinished. Writing it challenged me in more ways than one. And don't get me wrong, I love a challenge, but this one I found myself avoiding often. As I wrote each of these pieces, I was placed back into those spaces. The rooms, the people, the smells, the thoughts, the feelings. My body held it all for me. It needed to be processed and released. While writing, I realized I go through similar situations and thoughts in my life now, but I am better able to handle them.

As I came to understand my story, I knew it would impact others when I shared it. I didn't know how, and I didn't know it would come so soon. It wasn't until I read it out loud to a couple of audiences that I understood my story could truly touch someone else in the ways that I'd hoped.

I can't say that I am completely beyond suicidal ideation. To this day, I still struggle with it from time to time—the difference is that now I trust myself to keep myself safe. So, when those thoughts and feelings come up, and the weight of existence feels all-consuming, I feel it. I allow myself to really feel it. *What's heavy? Where in my body am I holding that weight? Do I have space for this? Can I make space for this? Do I need to call someone? Do I trust myself?* Questions and thoughts and images do and will come up. I let them go by. They aren't meant to stay. I am. Somatic work has been huge in my journey. I've come to be friends with my body, understand what it's saying, tend to my needs when troubling thoughts resurface, and take care of myself in the ways I now know how to. Learning my body has been like learning another language. I've changed the way I speak and think about things through talk therapy with counselors, opening my mind through seeking out new experiences and engaging others, and journaling (both audiovisual and written).

I've learned to be my best friend and biggest advocate, and to never allow myself to feel like I need to carry it all alone. Reaching out to my friend in March 2020 changed my life and perspective. I've gone through cycles of codependency, where leaning on people and substance was something I could not live without. That was a part of my learning too. Now I know I got me *and* others got me as well. I just know whom to lean on first. I know what it's like to feel like I'm carrying it all.

It's lighter now.

carry it all.

OPPOSITE
Jesus Ruiz, Untitled

DADDY'S GIRL

Arielle Effenberger

It's June 15, 2017. Graduation day. From where I'm standing, in line with the other graduates in the hallway behind the gym, I've seen my whole family show up—except for my dad. I told him I didn't want him coming if he couldn't show up sober. Now I'm fuming, tears welling up, because, once again, he put the bottle first.

My mind is racing.

How can I be mad at him for listening to my wishes? Not mad, no. Devastated. Why isn't he here? I don't care if he's drunk, I just want him here. Why does it always come down to the liquor? Why can't I be more important?

It is time for us to walk into the gym. My head is a cloud, and my legs are lead. All I can think about is whether he will show up. I put on a smile and try to focus on getting to my seat without stumbling. Once I'm there, I do a scan of the crowd and let out a sigh of relief, relaxing slightly, when my eyes land on him.

Not absent, just late.

His face is beet red, a sign he has been drinking on top of the already warm day. He's grinning from ear to ear, and I can see the boozy glisten in his eyes from across the aisle. He is wearing his usual faded light-blue jeans, white New Balance shoes, and white T-shirt. The real kicker is what's *on* it. He is wearing a shirt that his girlfriend bought him for Father's Day that says "#1 Dad."

I roll my eyes and audibly scoff. "What a joke," I mumble under my breath.

When the ceremony ends and we begin our final walk down the aisle that splits the audience in half, I see my dad pull one of my best friends, Sarah—who is about fifteen people in front of me—in for a hug. When the whole gym full of people lets out an audible "awww," my face turns as red as my dad's. It takes everything in me not to freeze in my tracks. I am clenching my fists so hard they're pure white, and I'm fighting back a wall of tears. Not because he hugged her—she is a sister to me—but because everyone was only seeing the sweet moment, and not the story or person behind it.

My dad is not a bad guy, by any means. He tries his best, but he isn't winning any "Father of the Year" awards. My time comes to exit, and as I pass him, he pulls me in for a hug, too. He says something, but the gym is too loud. All I can focus on is the stench of rum mixed with Listerine.

I should be happy he made an effort.

But right now, the feeling of betrayal is most prominent.

We head outside and into the cafeteria to be with our families, but I don't see my dad anywhere. Anxiety comes flooding back through my veins. My body and mind are busy sharing hugs, laughs, and niceties, while my eyes are searching frantically for him.

He finally pops up out of the crowd, heading back from the direction of the parking lot, which means he was taking a shot and having a cigarette. Then I notice that he's not smiling anymore. I see him mumbling under his breath.

He's about to tell me he isn't staying.

He notices me eyeing him, and the drunken grin returns to his face, though not quite ear to ear. He leans in to scoop me into a bear hug and says, "I'm so proud of you, Half Pint." He hands me some flowers and a card, then quickly says, "I gotta run, Princess, I'm sorry. I have to go help close the stand." I stand there for a moment, just blinking and trying to focus on not causing a scene.

"Okay," I say, blankly. "I get it. Thanks for coming."

His white T-shirt disappears into the crowd, and I feel like I'm going under water. My ears are muffled and there is a faint ringing. Not only does the liquor come before me on the most monumental day of my life, but so does his girlfriend and her coffee stand. Double whammy. He knows how hard I worked for this. He knows that not only did I have to take a second senior year, but that I almost didn't pass this one, either. He knows that working at that stand is a huge reason why I even had to take a second year to begin with. Now he's ditching me on graduation day to be with her. I'm not sure how I expected today to go, but this wasn't it.

When I open the card, I can tell he bought it last-minute, and that he was very drunk when he wrote it. His writing is scribbled and words are misspelled. I think it's supposed to say "I'm so proud of you! I love you, Half Pint!" but it looks more like "I'n SO RROUD OF YOU!! ILOVE YOU! HALF PINT!" The letters are overlapping, and there are scribbles on the card like the pen was running out of ink.

Once again I try to shake it off and enjoy my time with the family that did show up, and share some tears and laughs with my two best friends, Sarah and Danika. This whole year we've had each other to lean on, so I try to focus on them and every other person who helped me get to this point.

At first, focusing on my gratitude helps.

Then, it hurts.

I wish I could be grateful for my dad, but all he's done is shown me exactly who I don't want to be.

~ • ~

A few months after graduation, one of my good friends moves in with my boyfriend, Justin, and me. She graduated a year earlier, so it's fun at first, getting to reconnect as adults. But I'm realizing how much she reminds me of my father. She drinks all the time and has no limits, and she doesn't try to hide it; she's pretty shameless. It amazes me how much she can put away, because she's a very tiny person. She's a book you shouldn't judge by its cover, because you'd be totally wrong.

Nearly every day she's home, I wake up to her standing over

me—grinning mischievously with lifeless eyes—holding some sort of alcohol, saying "It's Modelo time, Foo!" I've never been good at saying "no," or setting boundaries, and she's heavy on the peer pressure. "Don't be a pussy, it's 5 o'clock somewhere! Just have a beer with me! C'mooonnn! Pussy, pussy, pussy! Don't be a little bitch! Justin can't get mad at you, you're a grown-ass adult! Just have one!"

I *could* say no. But that's never an option with her. If I say no, she'll just keep getting right in my face and calling me a "pussy." Which isn't the worst thing, but she's in my home, so giving in to the peer pressure is the easier battle. That's the one I pick.

The grin on her face grows as she realizes my defeat, and her eyes get even darker. I groan and reach out my hand to meet the beer that's in hers. She has beautiful, dainty hands and slender fingers. They make accepting the drink just slightly more enticing.

This is why hand models exist.

I drink the first beer in under fifteen minutes, and it doesn't stop there. We finish the six-pack, then go next door to the Shell station where they won't card us to get more.

Cheap beer, cheap wine, cheap liquor. Day in and day out. I've tried all kinds of alcohol in the past, even to the point of blacking out. But now, living with her, it's become a regular thing.

~ • ~

A month later, I'm applying to work at the nightclub where my roommate works. I've always been a homebody, not really one for crowds, introverted, and riddled with debilitating anxiety. The booming music, flashing lights, and crowd of people make me shake in my boots.

I'm sitting in the break room trying to ground myself, when she comes in with a water bottle full of vodka. "Just take a shot! That's what I do. You literally won't be anxious anymore."

She is right. After one shot, every ounce of anxiety in my body is gone. The fluttering in my stomach, heart, and head has turned into wings, and I feel like a social butterfly. I can talk to anyone about anything, I'm selling drinks left and right. I'm cracking jokes and laughing with customers. People are tipping me like crazy. I feel like I can climb to the top of the world ten times over.

Until I don't.

I go to find my friend to get another shot, but the bottle is empty. Waves of anxiety come crashing back down, and my wings return to their home as stomach, heart, and head. It is 1:00 in the morning, and the gas station next door is still open, so we send one of the bouncers to grab us a couple of cheap bottles of wine for the rest of the night. Once my cup is full, the flutters turn back into wings.

I am off to use my newfound superpower again.

~ • ~

November 22, 2017. My 20th birthday.

It feels like a repeat of graduation. I don't hear from my dad all day, then he finally sends a text saying he's going to come over to see me. He pulls up in the green Yukon, but leaves the engine running. He hops out quickly, wearing his usual white T-shirt, faded light-blue jeans, white New Balance shoes, and leather jacket. He runs over to me, card in hand, and gives me a half hug.

"Do you want to come in for a bit?" I ask, choking on the hope I know he is about to crush.

"I wish I could, Half Pint," he says, "but I have to go help at the stand. I love you. Happy Birthday!" He turns and runs back to his truck.

He doesn't seem too drunk right now, but it's always on his breath. I hate that he drives like this. I hate that I finally got my dad back—after years of seeing him only sporadically—and now he belongs to someone else. It's pouring down rain, and I'm glad, because it's masking the tears rolling down my face as he speeds out of my narrow driveway.

I walk back inside and my roommate silently extends her

arm, beer in hand. I chug that one, crack a second, and sit down to read the card. Same deal as with graduation . . . purchased last-minute, and scribbled, drunk handwriting.

Little to no thought.

I turn to the bottle for comfort.

~ • ~

It's Christmas day and I'm feeling painfully nostalgic. I haven't enjoyed Christmas, or any holiday, since my grandma's passing five years ago. She was what made them fun. She was the magic. When I was little, my dad's job and addiction left him mostly absent from my life, so my grandma would get me presents and say they were from him, just so I wouldn't know he had forgotten or couldn't afford to buy them himself. He was always confused when I would call him to thank him.

She went above and beyond to keep the pieces of our family together. Sometimes I wish she'd just been honest.

My grandparents' house is completely different without her: dark, gloomy, lacking color and life, and my grandpa's memory has been fading. Holidays now just feel like a sad attempt at bringing back a life that has parted from this world. Fewer and fewer people show up every year, and I am haunted by the emptiness of it all.

I should be happy to see everyone.

But everything about the day feels depressing. I haven't even left my apartment, and I'm already drinking to try and smother the anxiety I'm feeling about seeing my dad. I add a few shots of Crown Royal to the iced tea I'm sipping, then pour the rest of the bottle into a to-go cup to take with me.

I take a Snapchat video, caption it "this is how I'm surviving Christmas with my family" with a laugh, and send it to some friends.

When I arrive, my favorite cousin is there. We go outside to the patio by the hot tub for a smoke sesh, and I share my bottle of "tea." Everyone is drinking and chatting while we wait for dinner. I hear my dad's truck pull up, so my cousin and I load another bowl to smoke before he comes in. We shuffle inside right as my dad opens the front door. The smoke alarm makes its "chirp chirp chirp" and dad yells "knock knock"—his signature entrance.

I'm still hurt from my birthday, but I go over to hug him. I let him take a shot from my cup, because I can tell that today is just as hard for him as it is for me.

In a tone stiffer than the drink, he says "Thanks, Kid. Love you."

I go back outside with my cousin and let my dad make his rounds. Dinner is ready shortly after, so we all head to the table. My cousin and I pass the water bottle of whiskey back and forth under the table while the elder relatives argue about politics. We have enough of the fighting after about an hour and return to our smoke spot.

When the dishes are done, we exchange gifts. Dad's present for me is a bracelet that reads, "The love between a father and daughter is forever." I know I should feel happy; it's a sweet gift. But I'm still hurt from every time he's put the liquor before my brother and me. Not just the liquor, but also his girlfriend. I know she picked this out for him to give to me, and that makes it even worse. Why would a gift from the cause of 75% of our problems be a good idea? He knows I know his gift-giving style, and this isn't it.

I am seeing—and turning—red. I take back-to-back shots. My stomach is on fire, and I can't tell if it's the liquor or the rage.

By the end of the night, the whiskey is gone, and I'm ready to go home. As soon as I'm there, I pop open another fifth. I can't sit still; anxiety, pain, and liquor courses through my veins. Justin goes to sleep and I get called into work. It's snowing heavily by now, so I'm not sure I'll make it, but I try anyway. Anywhere is better than sitting with my feelings.

Once I'm in the Uber, we get half a mile from my apartment when the car gets stuck on an icy hill and hits another car. I go to call my dad for help, but my phone is dead. I have no option but to walk home in the deep snow and ice. It's not that far, but after the day I've had, every slippery crunch of my feet makes me feel as physically unstable as I am mentally.

I make it back home after an hour of slipping, sliding, crunching, falling. I am sopping wet and freezing cold.

I decide to warm up the best way I know.

I drink.

~ • ~

Three weeks later, it's my dad's birthday.

I anxiously twiddle my phone in my hand all day long, debating whether to call. I don't want to be mean, but I also want him to feel how I felt.

By dinnertime, I settle on a text.

Happy Birthday, Dad. I love you.

It's simple. Too simple, coming from me. I know he will feel that. I almost feel bad for sending anything at all if I'm not in a place to be extra loving and kind. But I know he'll be happy to hear from me.

My phone buzzes.

Thank you, Half Pint. Love you! I know things have been rough for us and I want to get coffee when I'm back in town to talk about it. By the way, I haven't had a drink since the day I went into the hospital, and I haven't had more than two cigarettes a day since Saturday.

It's a much better response than I expected. He was in the hospital for gall and kidney stones a few weeks earlier, and we have all been harping on him about his health ever since.

I sit for a minute and think about what to say back. I settle on,

> I'm really glad to hear that, Dad. Seriously. Keep it up.

I know it's not enthusiastic or encouraging, but I can't help but think *I'll believe it when I see it.* I am hopeful, though. His girlfriend has caused a huge rift in our relationship and we're finally going to discuss it.

I can't wait for next week.

~ • ~

Two days later I pull into the parking lot of the Gourmet Latte where I work and do one last check of my notifications before my shift starts. I go on Instagram, where I see a message from my cousin Monique.

It reads, "Arielle I need u to msg me ASAP!!"

"What's wrong, Boo?" I respond.

"Can u call me?"

"I'm at work rn I can't make a call. Are you okay??"

"I got a msg from a social worker and it's about your dad. He had a heart attack while driving and she can't get ahold of anyone so she messaged me cause we have the same last name. She can't make any calls about what to do because she needs a family member to say it's okay. I'll give you her number, he's in the trauma unit."

My heart drops to my gut. I am sweating and shaking, tears are welling up in my eyes. My dad has been working in Eastern Washington, so it's a three-hour drive minimum to get there.

Is he already gone? Do I have any time left at all?

I'm trying to hold it together to make the phone call.

The social worker answers, and I state my name, my dad's name and date of birth, and that I am his daughter. She confirms that he had a heart attack while driving and connects me to the doctor working on his case. I run inside the stand, bawling and gasping for air, to tell my coworker what happened and that I can't stay. The doctor picks up and confirms what the social worker and my cousin told me.

I ask, begging, "Is he alive?"

Long pause.

The doctor says, "He is stable."

I collapse against the door of the stand and fall to the floor. I know what that means. I know they can't say anything else until I'm there in person.

I run out of the stand and call my mom. I explain as best I can what just happened, and she tells me to get a bag together and she will come get me. Every second feels like an hour. I'm chain-smoking, but I avoid drinking because I know I need to be sober for what's coming. When she whips into the parking lot, I run to the car, hop in, and we race north to get my little brother from school.

Oh, my god. My brother. What are we going to tell him? Will he understand?

When he gets in the car, he asks, "Is dad going to be okay?" in his tiny, worried voice.

I feel like I'm going to vomit.

We have to go south to go east because of traffic, and as we pass the exit to my grandparents' home—the last home I shared with my father—my parents' wedding song comes on the radio: "I Hope You Dance" by Lee Ann Womack. The song that my mom would always sing to me, and the song my dad would tell me to listen to whenever I was going through a hard time. A song that rarely ever plays on the radio. My mom and I share an eerie look, and we fight back tears; it's a sign from my dad, telling us he won't be coming home.

We make it to the hospital in record time. No traffic, no tickets, no snow on the pass. We stop at the front desk for directions, run to the elevator, get in, and beg it to move faster. We make it to the trauma ICU floor and race out of the elevator to the front desk. They give us our passes, and we all but run to the room at the end of the hallway.

There he is.

He's hooked up to all kinds of tubes and machines. He is on life support, in a coma. Not sitting up, not cracking his goofy jokes. Just lying there.

I sink into his bed and sob, "My daddy."

~ • ~

The next morning, the doctors gather us into their private meeting room so they can update us on his condition. None of them look hopeful, and a few are fighting back tears themselves. They tell us they're sorry, but his brain is hemorrhaging and there is nothing else they can do to save him.

I slam my fists onto the table and let out a violent, gut-churning scream. "NOOOOO! NO NO NO NO NO! MY DADDY! MY DADDY! NO!"

I stand up and kick my chair to the floor, screaming more.

"Calm down," my dad's girlfriend says as she reaches for my shoulder.

I recoil. If looks could kill, my eyes could pierce her heart right then and there. My mom grabs me and holds me tightly. Any other day, it would've broken my bones, but today it's the only thing holding them together. We leave the room and I go back to my dad's bed to hold him for a while. His girlfriend follows soon after, so I step out for a cigarette.

When I come back inside, I have to sign his Do Not Resuscitate order because I'm next of kin. My aunt and mom hold me tight and reassure me that I'm doing what I have to and that this is what he would want, despite his girlfriend trying to guilt me into not signing it. As if this isn't hard enough. As if she isn't the worst thing to ever happen to him. I know what my dad would want, though. He has always said, "If I can't wipe my own ass, just put me out of my misery."

It takes me an hour and several breakdowns to finally sign.

After the paperwork, they have to take him off of life support to see if he can breathe on his own. We all wait in stunned, eerie silence—too silent for a hospital—hoping for a miracle. But nothing happens. The machines start beeping to alert the doctors that his pulse and oxygen levels are dangerously low. My mom, aunt, brother, stepsister, best friend Sarah, and I let out a sob. We all know what that means.

The doctors turn the sounds off on the machines and give us a moment to collect ourselves before announcing, "He is brain-dead."

Watching his lack of movement and hearing the beeping as a result was enough to confirm this, but hearing those words spoken out loud makes it real.

I can't contain myself. The noises coming out of me are too big for my quivering body to hold back. Every wail is a thunderclap, echoing off the walls. I try to focus on collecting myself so I can exit the room without making a scene for the other patients.

I need some air.

Because he is an organ donor, they put him back on life support to keep everything preserved. My mom, aunt, and I go sit in the family room to give our other loved ones some time with him. My aunt hands me her bottle of Pure Leaf tea, which isn't tea at all. I don't realize until I take a sip that it's whiskey, but I'm thankful once the burn hits my throat.

We pass the bottle around for a while, then return to dad's room to soak up whatever time is left.

~ • ~

Later that night, the hospital provides us with blankets, clay and paint for handprints, and other little trinkets of memorabilia. We write him notes and a donor acknowledgment that will be read over him before removing his organs. We tell stories about him, laugh, and cry.

At the end of the night, we walk him to the operating room.

It's a slow walk. I beg every second to be longer. I know that once we get downstairs, I will never see his face again. The elevator reaches basement level, and I freeze. I don't want to get out. But we have to. We walk him to the double doors, and I give him one last kiss.

"We have to take him now, I'm so sorry," says one of the doctors.

I watch as they cart him through the doors. Once they swing shut, I collapse on the floor in front of them and sob for some time. My mom pulls me up, and we go back to the motel where my stepsister and I drink ourselves to sleep.

It's after midnight, maybe even well into the night. My brain and eyes are fuzzy from the days of crying and drinking.

My mom is trying to wake me. "Ari, it's time," she says.

It's time. I'm not ready for this. I wasn't ready for any of this.

But it doesn't matter. It's time.

I drag myself out of bed, every movement fighting the lead that has replaced my bones. Somehow, I make it to the car. We leave my brother at the motel with my stepsister; he doesn't want to be there for this part. I don't blame him. I don't want him to have to remember this.

We make it to the hospital for the last time, back to the OR, then begin to walk dad to the hearse. The nurse turns down the wrong hallway, so we have to walk through an emergency room full of staring, offended eyes as we cart the bulky, black, zipped up body bag past them as quickly as possible. Everyone is mortified. I want to scream at them all "LOOK AWAY! MIND YOUR BUSINESS!" but I hold back. It's not their fault he's dead, or that they're sick, or that the nurse took a wrong turn. I wish it was. I wish I had someone to blame. We finally make it outside where the hearse is waiting.

I can't tell if I'm shivering from the cold weather or my fear. I think it's both. My mom, aunt, and I ask the driver for a few minutes to say our final goodbyes.

I lay my head across my dad's chest—where I presume it

would be—one last time. I try to speak, but all that escapes my mouth is garbled sobs. I yell out one last “I LOVE YOU” as the driver closes the hatch.

“I am so sorry for your loss,” he says, then gets in the driver’s seat and closes the door.

I collapse, once again, as the hearse drives away with my daddy. I let out a scream and kick the concrete block closest to me.

My mom scoops me up into a hug and says, “It’s time to go. We have to leave now. I’m so sorry, Baby.”

Tomorrow there will be no hospital, no room to come back to. This journey is over. His journey is over. His *life* is over.

Mine feels over too.

~ • ~

Winter: An Open Letter to My Father

Maybe one day, I’ll be able to enjoy the twinkling lights, warm smells, cheerful music, glistening snow, and crisp air in my lungs.
For now, they all remind me of the fifth of whiskey that got me through our last Christmas and how we argued the whole time.
How you gave me that bracelet and how my stomach boiled with rage, because at the time, our relationship was anything but loving.
How I drank even more when I got home.
And I realized—I couldn’t be angry at you—because I was you.
How we made plans to have coffee and make amends for your birthday.
How I lost you forever
just a few
short
weeks
later.

And how
I never got to say
Goodbye.

Now, that bracelet is one of the last things I have left of you
and I can only wish I'd been kinder when you gave it to me.
That I'd realized—it was your way of apologizing—of saying
"You will always be my little Half Pint. You will always be
Daddy's Girl."

I wish I could feel winter in my bones without it shattering them like glass.
I wish there was a way to melt them back together that wasn't the fire of liquor in my veins.
I wish I had some way to feel connected to you—to really understand you—that wasn't the bottom of the bottle, or running from everyone who loves me
because I'm so afraid I'll hurt them the ways I've hurt myself.

For now, the white-capped trees and icy roads just remind me of your brutal end
and a lifetime of regrets.
I wish winter didn't hurt so bad.

Maybe it will take me next.

A NOTE FROM ARIELLE

I started writing this story over seven years ago, during my first senior year at Scriber Lake High School. At the time, my relationship with my dad was so tumultuous that I just couldn't bring myself to finish. After he passed away, I spent the better part of five years diving headfirst into my own addiction. I had already been drinking heavily for a few months prior to his death, but that is ultimately what threw me in full force. Alcohol, cocaine, and various pills were a part of my daily life. I wasn't always drunk and high, but once I started for the day, there was no stopping. I tried going to meetings and befriending sober people. I tried therapy, intensive outpatient, partial hospitalization, and full hospitalization. I'd go on the wagon, then fall off days later. I tried "drinking in moderation," but that never worked and almost always led to other drugs. It took many failed attempts, developing an alcohol allergy, ruining several relationships, and ultimately hitting rock bottom's basement for me to really take sobriety seriously. My longest time sober was 43 days. Until now. As of today, June 20, 2023, I am one year and 29 days clean and sober. I have a beautiful, wonderful group of people that I have the privilege of calling family—most of whom are not blood—but without them, I simply would not have made it this far. In the fall of 2022, I reached out to Marjie to tell her I wanted to go back to school, and she told me she could help me with that—as long as I finished my story. I trashed the dozens of rough drafts and bits of scratch paper I had from years prior and started over entirely. I stared blankly at my laptop screen, willing the words to come out—and they did. In one eight-hour sitting, I pumped out a new story—this story—from scratch. I am now a substitute paraeducator at Scriber, and I am aiming for a future position in the counseling department. I hope to begin school in the fall to work on accomplishing this goal. For this opportunity, I have to thank Bob Fuller, a man who is no longer with us, but whose legacy will live on forever in the hearts of every student he was so generous to help in their darkest hour. Bob helped me with bills and hand-delivered flowers and cards to my apartment after I lost my dad. He was a huge supporter of Steep Stairs Press and its mission. Now that I am "on the other side," I am able to see that I'm still my Daddy's Girl, even without the booze. His character shines through me every day. I have his goofiness, wit, sarcasm, morbid sense of humor, drive, and willingness to help anyone who should need it. He was the type of person that would pull over on the side of the road to use jumper cables on a stranger's car, give them a tow, or even manually push their vehicle up a hill. I can recall several times where he literally gave the shirt off his back to someone who needed it more. I can now see that addiction is only a very small part of what I share with my father, though I understood him more through battling my own. You never really know, until you do. Then you *really* do. It is a never-ending battle, but it's one I am so grateful to fight. I miss my dad every single moment, and I will always be upset that we aren't on this journey together. Every moment I spend sober is for him, for the both of us. One of the hardest parts about his death is that his attempt at getting sober is what ended his life. The problem wasn't sobriety itself, it was that he had spent most of his life as an addict, and he went from drinking and drugging to great extremes every day to essentially trying to go cold turkey, which shocked his system. If you are a recovering addict, please make sure that you take the proper steps. Sometimes medical intervention is absolutely necessary, so please use that resource if you have it. Our bodies are all different and react to withdrawal in different ways. However you go about your own journey, know that you are not alone and that every step forward is one you should be incredibly proud of.

"God, grant me the serenity to accept the things I cannot change, courage to change the things I can, and wisdom to know the difference."
—The Serenity Prayer

OPPOSITE
Jasper Rhodes, Today I Find Joy

Today I find Joy
in being recognized.
Allow
yourself,
To
look.

OH HOW I LOVE BEING A WOMAN

Jasper Rhodes

When I was little, I never thought about gender. I was just me
until I realized that meant something different
to everyone else around me.
I was a girl because they told me I was—not because it felt
right to me.
And I love the parts of me that came from being raised a girl.
From being my mother's oldest daughter.
But I can't embrace those parts of myself without people telling
me it means I don't know who I am.

I love kids, I love holding babies and being emotional and
wearing skirts.
But I don't live in one box.
I am not a Woman
and I don't understand why certain interests and characteristics
negate that statement.

I'm thankful for how I was raised.
I wouldn't want to see the world in a different way.
The view I've looked through every day since I was a little girl
has shaped me into the person I am today.

Maybe I don't wish I was different.
Maybe I just wish they would let me exist without constantly questioning me.
I don't wish I was cis—but there is such a burden in being trans.
I carry this weight with me
every
day.
It holds me down
and I drag my feet with every step.
Every time I look in the mirror it feels like a fire is lit in my chest
and it eats up all my air until I choke on my own
nothing
that is left.

I feel trapped
trapped in my body
trapped by their words and opinions I never asked for.

Sometimes it makes me want to scream.
It makes me want to rip my hair out.
I become overwhelmed with the urge to scream.
To bang on the walls, to hit myself, to cry.

And I know none of that will do anything.
I can't get rid of the fire in my chest and it will keep sucking the oxygen out of me until I suffocate.

So do you get it now?

Probably not.
You'll never feel the burn for yourself.
Never know how it is to be something so hated, by them
and yourself.

I don't need you to tell me I don't know who I am
to tell me I'll change my mind.
I'm asking for your support.

I'm falling apart along the same seams I re-sewed years ago
when I had my first preteen growth spurt and realized I no
    longer belonged here,
stuck beneath skin I wore like a mask fitted too tight.

I've held on to pieces of her
pieces of the girl I once was.
I've kept her with me.

I'll always have her and love her
but she's not me anymore.
And I can't ever go back to pretending she is.

A NOTE FROM JASPER

I wrote this poem to capture my experience of being transgender and how it has affected how people see me and how I see myself. I wrote it to process the complicated feelings I have about my transition and how it has affected my relationships.

I entered the WeSpeak competition at the Edmonds Center for the Arts hoping to share my message with a larger audience. I wanted to give other trans kids something to relate to and to offer insight to people in those kids' lives that may not understand what they're going through.

After being awarded a finalist position for WeSpeak, I completed a few workshops with two other finalists. These workshops helped me get comfortable with sharing my poetry and honing my performance skills. It created a really unique sense of community for me that I haven't felt anywhere else.

Performing on stage with writer and poet Anastacia-Reneé was a surreal, life-changing experience. She is an incredibly passionate and kind person, and she made us feel welcome, supported, and equally important.

I feel I am on the right path with my writing. I now want more exposure to the spoken word scene, and my dream is to someday compile my poetry and publish it. To create is to be seen—to be seen by those you never thought cared to look. To create is to bare your soul and prepare for however it may be received.

carry it all.

Jesus Ruiz, Untitled

A NOTE FROM JESUS RUIZ

Ever since I can remember, I have had a passion for and connection to art. My art has grown exponentially over the years through overcoming many challenges: my dad getting deported when I was very young, and my mom's struggles with mental health issues, which eventually led to her death. I moved through multiple houses until my grandmother adopted me and my two sisters about nine years ago. Through the constant changes in my environment, art has been my coping mechanism.

Last year, I was at the lowest point in my life. I was finally processing all my emotions, and it was a very confusing time. In the midst of that, I decided I would try to be more confident with my art. I started posting my work to social media and, after receiving positive feedback, I got inspired to continue sharing it in other places. I entered the school talent show, which led to a request to do the cover of the 2023 Scriber yearbook, which then led to being asked to be the artist for *I Used to Carry It All*.

I can relate to this title in a very personal way. After a very long period of loneliness, I became tired of the cycle of keeping to myself and started taking every chance to put myself out there. I began telling people how I felt and was honest about what was holding me back. The most important part is that I realized I could never and will never be able to do it alone. The only reason I am still here is because of the amazing people in my life who genuinely care about me and have been there when I needed them. Today I can say that I like being myself and that everything good has flowed from that place of self-acceptance.

Everything improves when you stop trying to be somebody you aren't and find people who love you because of who you are. Art has fueled my creativity, allowed me to connect with others, and helped me develop new and meaningful relationships with people who truly believe that I can do something special.

My process for creating the art featured in this book was one of complete trial and error. This is the first time I've worked on a project like this, so getting it right was very important to me. I wanted to create art that was personal and unique to my story, but at first each idea felt unrelated to the rest. Any time I visualized what I've personally had to carry, it always tied back to my family. For the first time in years, I decided to look through old family photos taken when I was much younger. I wasn't sure if I was going to use them as references or not, but I knew that looking through them and thinking about how they made me feel could help my direction. I immediately gravitated toward photos of my mother, which was like looking into a whole other world at a woman I barely knew—a person who put the closest people she knew through a lot of pain. I also saw a scared young woman who was raised by the same cycles of neglect and abuse that ended up leading her down a road that no human being should ever have to endure.

The people who raise us shape us with their own fears, desires, and needs. In my own life, I can see how these things took away from what I could've been if they had never happened. I am beginning to understand all of this.

I am now hopeful for my future. I want to attend college and work to not only improve my artistic skills, but also to develop a better understanding of other subjects that will help me on my journey.

carry it all.

ACKNOWLEDGMENTS

We owe a debt of gratitude to our Edmonds community for its support since this writing program began in 2011. We are lucky to live in such a compassionate "village" where so many individuals take a special interest in our kids on a daily basis. Here are some highlights:

Within a year of our first publication in 2012, three men we came to refer to as "The Three Musketeers" emerged as champions of our writing program: Rock Roth of the Edmonds Daybreakers Rotary, Bob Fuller of the Lynnwood Rotary, and George Murray of the Edmonds Kiwanis. Rock passed away in 2014, Bob passed away in 2020, and George passed away in 2021. We appreciate how each man's respective club has stepped in to support us in their absence.

We have been gifted with many unexpected supporters over the years. Seattle Public Theater partnered with us on the stage beginning in 2013. Trudy Catterfeld taught us how to become professional publishers in 2016. Scarlet Parke and Dimiter Yordanov brought music to our stories in 2018. Haifa Fakih Alhussieni of Café Louvre has graciously hosted our book releases since 2013 and spearheaded moving the event to the Edmonds Waterfront Center to host a larger audience this year. The people at Edmonds Bookshop have carried our books since the beginning. And the Edmonds Lutheran Church won't stop finding generous ways to demonstrate creative, consistent support.

Tim Holsopple took over all publishing responsibilities for our last two books: the copyediting, the cover design, the interior layout, the production . . . everything!

We are in awe of how each gift has deepened and expanded our program.

The Edmonds School District maintains its support in all ways, with special thanks to Scriber Principal Mike Piper for his compassionate leadership.

Our greatest thanks, however, go to the Scriber writers' parents, who show so much courage in supporting their children.

We are grateful.

ABOUT THE EDITOR

Marjie Bowker has taught English and a little history somewhere in the world (including China, Norway, and Vietnam) for the past 23 years, in addition to her "regular" spot at Scriber. She is a cofounder of Steep Stairs Press and is the author of two curriculum guides, *They Absolutely Want to Write: Teaching the Heart and Soul of Narrative Writing* and *Hippie Boy Teaching Guide: Transforming Lives through Personal Storytelling*, and a book based on the concepts of Appreciative Inquiry, *Creating a Success Culture: Transforming Our Schools One Question at a Time.*

ABOUT SCRIBER LAKE HIGH SCHOOL

Scriber Lake High is a public school of approximately 150 students in the Edmonds School District, located just north of Seattle. We are one of Washington's oldest alternative schools. Scriber is a school of choice; some students come to us as freshmen, and some come seeking a second, third, or fourth chance to graduate. A majority of our students have struggled with depression, anxiety, abuse, loss, homelessness, or drugs and alcohol, and have been lost in the educational system because of these outside factors.

In 2012, our staff accepted a three-year challenge to increase our students' sense of self-efficacy and resiliency through the use of Appreciative Inquiry questioning techniques. Under the leadership of Dr. Cal Crow, Director of the Center for Efficacy and Resiliency, we challenged ourselves to create a school filled with heart and soul—a school focused on supporting students' stories and dreams for the future.

In 2015, we published a book about our journey called *Creating a Success Culture: Transforming Our Schools One Question at a Time.* It features anecdotal stories of how we changed conversations with our students to bring them back into the center of their own education. We invite conversations with other schools working to address the needs of students impacted by childhood trauma.

OPPOSITE
Jesus Ruiz, Untitled

I

used

to

Printed in the USA
CPSIA information can be obtained
at www.ICGtesting.com
CBHW072052080424
6599CB00003B/5

9 780997 472448